The Far Western Frontier

The Far Western Frontier

Advisory Editor

RAY A. BILLINGTON

Senior Research Associate
at the Henry E. Huntington Library
and Art Gallery

TRIP

TO THE

WEST AND TEXAS

A[MOS] A[NDREW] PARKER

ARNO PRESS

A NEW YORK TIMES COMPANY

New York • 1973

Reprint Edition 1973 by Arno Press Inc.

Reprinted from a copy in The State
Historical Society of Wisconsin Library

The Far Western Frontier
ISBN for complete set: 0-405-04955-2
See last pages of this volume for titles.

Manufactured in the United States of America

Publisher's Note: This volume was reprinted
from the best available copy.

Library of Congress Cataloging in Publication Data

Parker, Amos Andrew, 1791-1893.
   Trip to the West and Texas.

   (The Far Western frontier)
   Reprint of the 1835 ed.
   1. Mississippi Valley--Description and travel.
2. Texas--History--Revolution, 1835-1836. 3. Texas
--Description and travel. I. Title. II. Series.
F353.P23 1973   917.3   72-9463
ISBN 0-405-04991-9

TRIP

TO THE

WEST AND TEXAS

Catching wild horses.

TRIP

WEST AND TEXAS.

COMPRISING

A JOURNEY OF EIGHT THOUSAND MILES,

THROUGH

NEW-YORK, MICHIGAN, ILLINOIS, MISSOURI, LOUISIANA AND
TEXAS, IN THE AUTUMN AND WINTER OF
1834—5.

INTERSPERSED WITH ANECDOTES, INCIDENTS
AND OBSERVATIONS.

BY A. A. PARKER.

———

PRINTED AND PUBLISHED BY WHITE & FISHER.

1835.

PREFACE.

THE AUTHOR of this work, unknown to fame, and unacquainted with the art of book-making, has endeavored, in the following pages, to give some account of the great WESTERN AND SOUTHERN COUNTRY. In performing this task, he has not attempted the regions of fancy and fiction; but has told his own story—" a plain unvarnished tale," in his own way, without reference to books or other travellers. And although it may not indicate much depth of research, or possess all the graces of polished diction and charms of novelty, yet he hopes it may be found to contain information sufficient to repay a perusal.

He spent five months on his journey, and examined the country through which he passed, as much as time would permit:—Its soil, climate and productions—the manners, customs and health of the inhabitants—the animals, reptiles and insects—in short, all things favorable and unfavorable in the NEW WORLD. He has freely spoken of the country just as it appeared to him; and he believes the infor-

mation this work purports to give, may be safely re-
lied upon. But if it should be found to contain er-
rors of fact, or of opinion, he is confident they will
be deemed unintentional.

It would have been quite easy to make a much
larger book of the author's travels; and had he followed the example set him by some of the journal-
ists of the day, he should have done so. But his
object was not to make a large and expensive volume. He has given, in a concise form, such descriptions, incidents and anecdotes only, as he believes
may instruct and amuse, and enable the public to
form a correct opinion of the country. How he
has succeeded in his undertaking, others, of course,
will judge for themselves; but he hopes this little
work may be found not entirely destitute of useful
and entertaining matter, and prove an acceptable
offering to his friends and fellow-citizens.

EXETER, N. H. 1835.

A TRIP

WEST AND TEXAS.

In September, 1834, I left Exeter, New-Hampshire, for the purpose of visiting the Western States and Texas. Although public attention had been for some time directed thither, by various published sketches and frequent emigration; yet so little was definitely known, that I was induced to travel through these sections of the country to learn their actual situation and condition. My object was not to visit the settled regions of the country, a full knowledge of which may be obtained from books, but to see some portion of the unknown and unsettled regions of the West and the South. My particular attention was, therefore, directed to Michigan, Illinois, Missouri, Louisiana and Texas.

But so rapidly are some portions of this new country settling; so constantly are new villages

springing up in the wilderness; and so continually
are improvements making, that history must continue to lag behind the reality. To keep any thing
like an even pace with population, and the public
constantly informed of the actual condition of the
country, would require, like an almanac, an annual
revision and publication of its history.

I took passage on board the stage, through Brat-
tleborough and Bennington, to Albany. About a
dozen years ago, I travelled over this route, and was
gratified to find so many improvements in the villages, farms, and especially in the stage road, since
I had travelled it before. In passing through Vermont, I found a new road had been made to avoid
the high hills over which it formerly passed, so that
now, I believe this is the easiest and safest route
across the Green mountains.

Two opposition turnpikes were almost completed from Bennington to Troy—one entering at the
upper, the other at the lower part of the city. The
public have been badly accommodated in this quarter. The old road is rough, hilly and circuitous.—
One of the turnpikes would have been abundantly
sufficient; but if Troy chooses to make two, the
travelling public will not probably object. Opposition seems to be the order of the day; and although
it has caused much improvement in the ease and facility of travelling, yet it is often troublesome and
annoying. As we drove up to the door of the
stage house in Albany, an agent of one of the

steam-boats, thrust in his head and gave us a hand-bill of a boat—enquired if we were going down the river, and without waiting for an answer, said it was a good boat, swift, low pressure engine, start at nine in the morning, fare to New-York city only *fifty* cents. In the bar-room, we had to pass through the same ceremony with the agent of another boat; and I had to take a third edition in the street next morning.

The Erie canal terminates in a large basin, immediately on the banks of the Hudson river, so that the freight of the canal boats can be conveniently transferred to the river boats. Western travellers can here take passage on board the canal boat, or go on the railroad to Schenectady and take a boat there. But as the canal is twice the distance of the rail-road, travellers generally choose the latter.— Travellers from the North, when accompanied by their families and baggage, usually stop at Troy, and take a canal boat there, for the West.

The ancient city of Albany has the appearance of much business and wealth; and some portions of it are pleasant, especially, in the region of the State-house and other public buildings. From the river, the ground rapidly rises, so that the city stands upon the side of a hill, and makes a fine appearance, when viewed from the opposite shore.

The railroad commences in State street, a short distance below the State-house yard; and so steep is the ascent, that the cars are drawn for a mile by

horses. Here a steam engine was hitched on, and
we started off at a rapid rate. The distance from
Albany to Schenectady is sixteen miles, and we
travelled it over in less than an hour. Here we
were assailed by the agents and captains of the ca-
nal-boats, and those who could make the most noise
and bustle, and obtain the most passengers, were
the best fellows.

There are three kinds of boats in general use on
the canal. The Packet boats, drawn by three
horses, and go at the rate of about five miles an
hour. They are fitted up in good style, intended
exclusively for passengers and their baggage—having elegant cabins, drawing-rooms, berths, &c. Fare,
five cents a mile and found.

The Line boats—designed for freight and passengers also. These are drawn by two horses, and
travel at the rate of two and a half or three miles
an hour. The fare is one cent a mile for passage
only; and one and a half cents addition per mile,
for board. Families travelling to the West, generally take the Line boats. They can travel much
cheaper, than in any other mode. They furnish
their own provisions, and have the privilege of cooking on board the boat. Provisions are plenty and
cheap, and can be bought at almost every stopping
place, along the whole line of the canal.

And the Scows, used exclusively for grain, flour,
lumber, &c., which are employed by the farmers to
carry their own produce to market. These are

drawn by two horses; and many of them have two sets of horses, and stalls made on board to keep one set, while the other draw the boat; and at regular intervals, relieve each other. By this means, they keep the boat continually going, night and day.

The Packet boats ply between the large towns on the canal, from Schenectady to Utica; from Utica to Rochester, &c., so that a traveller, in going through the whole route, must shift his baggage and himself from one boat to another, three or four times. But the Line boats run the whole length of the canal, from Albany or Troy to Buffalo. These boats are furnished with horses by a company, who have them stationed at regular intervals of about twelve miles the whole distance.

All the boats, at night, carry two brilliant lights in the bow, so as to enable the helmsman to steer, and avoid other boats when they meet. I took passage on board one of the Troy and Erie line. I found good accommodations, and good company. In the forward part of the boat, were the gentlemen's and ladies' cabins; in the stern, the dining and cook rooms; and in the centre the place for freight. It was about seventy feet long, and eight or ten feet in width. Three other passengers, besides myself, went the whole route; a lady and her daughter from Pennsylvania, and a Dr. Warren of Rhode Island; and way-passengers were continually coming aboard, and leaving the boat, at our sev-

1*

eral stopping places. I found travelling on the canal pleasant, and in fine weather, delightful. We were continually passing villages, farms, locks, viaducts, or boats; and these, with the company aboard, afforded an agreeable variety. When I wished for exercise, I would jump ashore, and take a walk along the hard trod tow-path.

I was really surprised to find so many boats on the canal. We met them almost every mile, and sometimes, three or four together. The Line boats are owned by companies; and the captain told me that forty-five boats belonged to his line. When one happens to run aground, which is sometimes the case, when deeply laden and the water low, it is of course, in the centre of the canal; so that boats cannot pass on either side; in such an event, twenty or thirty boats will be congregated in a few hours.

The boats pass each other on the left hand side, and without trouble or delay. The whole process of passing belongs to the out side boat; or the one the farthest from the tow-path. All the inside boat has to do, is to steer near the tow-path, and keep on as usual. The out side boat hauls one way, and their horses the other, and lets the tow-rope slack, so that the inside horses and boat can pass over it, between them. The tow-path sometimes changes from one side to the other of the canal; and the horses are transferred by means of a bridge. They pass underneath the bridge, and turn up on to it, the further side; so as to keep the tow-rope clear of it. The riders display their horsemanship by whipping over these bridges at full speed. Accidents, however, sometimes occur.— One day, the Packet boat passed us, a short distance from a tow-path bridge; and as the horses were going at full speed across it, the forward one slipped, fell over the railing, and drew the others after him. The rider saved himself by leaping from the horse to the bridge. The two forward horses fell into the water, and came out uninjured; but the rear one fell across the edge of the tow-path and was killed on the spot.

The Erie canal is a great and noble work; and has gained a niche in the temple of fame, for its great founder. It has been of incalculable benefit to New-York, and the rising States in the West; and must continue to be, in all time to come. Now it is completed, and in successful operation, men may cease to wonder; but so improbable was it generally thought to be, to make such a long line of canal, on a route so difficult and expensive, that an intelligent gentleman informed me, that when he was asked by one of the surveyors, if he should not admire to see boats passing before his door; emphatically replied, if life was guaranteed till that event, he would then willingly resign it. A few years only passed, before the event did happen, but he is not yet *quite* willing to die.

It was indeed a great undertaking. None but a man of a gigantic mind, of steady purpose and firm resolution, could have conceived, planned and executed it. It all along bears the marks of so much labor and expense, that a common mind would have been deterred from making the attempt. The canal passes over an extent of country much more rough, broken and hilly than I had supposed. Long levels of canal are found to be sure; but they are made at great expense, by filling up deep gullies, winding round the side of hills, or deep cuts through them; and by walling up, by the side of streams, or aqueducts over them.

Every few miles, the canal passes through a village. Many of these have sprung into existence, since the completion of the canal; and others have much increased in size, wealth and beauty. They are all *ornamented* with grog-shops, containing, among other miscellaneous matter, an abundant supply of "boat-stores."

New-York has a great variety of romantic scenery. It has more beautiful and stupendous water-falls than any other State in the Union; and the lover of nature's choicest works might very pleasantly spend months in viewing them. *Trenton Falls*, on the West Canada Creek, a large stream that empties into the Mohawk, are situated about twenty four miles above its mouth. They consist of several *chutes* for the distance of two miles, commencing near Black river road, and terminating at Conrad's mills.

The upper fall is about twenty feet; and the descent above, for two miles, is not less than sixty feet.— The water, here compressed into a narrow space, is received into a large basin, rolls down a precipitous ravine a hundred feet in depth, and presents to the eye the most romantic peculiarities. Some of the topmost crags overhanging the stream; and here and there, a hardy tree, having gained a foot-hold in the crevices of the rock, throws its branches athwart the abyss. There are six distinct falls. The next below, are two pitches, called the *Cascades;* where the water falls eighteen feet—The Mill Dam Falls of thirteen feet.

The *High Falls*, consisting of three pitches— one of forty-eight; the second of eleven; and the third, of thirty-seven feet—*Sherman's Falls*, of thirty-five feet. The last fall is at Conrad's mills, and is only six feet; but the descent of water, from the top of the upper fall to the lower one, is three hundred and eighty-seven feet—and the whole forms as wild and romantic a scene as the enthusiastic lover of nature's most eccentric works could desire. Organic remains have been found in the ravine in abundance, and Mr. Sherman has a cabinet of them, which are exhibited to the curious.

Ithica Falls are situated at the head of Cayuga Lake. The high fall of Fall River is the first that strikes the eye, in going from the steam-boat landing to the village, and is one hundred and sixteen feet in height. Two immense piles of rocks enclose the stream. On the right hand high up the bluff, a mill race is seen winding around a point in the bank, suspended in mid air; and sometimes an adventurous visiter, may be seen cautiously wending his way along the dizzy path on the verge of the abyss! The mill race was built, by letting a man down over the giddy steep by a rope fastened to a tree above, who dug holes in the bluff, in which to fasten its principal supports. A short distance from this, up the rocky bed of the creek, is another splendid fall—not so high as the first, but more wild and beautiful. Above these, are three more falls, the upper one of which is the highest fall of water of any, and is the most grand and imposing. These four falls have a descent of four hundred and thirty-eight feet in the short distance of a mile, and present to the eye as great a variety of the romantic and beautiful in nature, as earth affords.

There are *Cascadilla, Six Mile Creek, Buttermilk Creek,* &c. &c. many romantic scenes and splendid falls; but it would interfere with the design of this work to stop to describe them. I cannot, however, leave the high falls on *Taghcanic Creek* without a passing notice. They are eight miles from Ithica, near a landing place, called Goodwin's point; and are two hundred and thirty-eight feet perpendicular! Who shall attempt to describe such a magnificent exhibition as this; or the effect it produces on the mind! This is said to be the favorite resort of parties of pleasure and lovers of the picturesque. And who, but the real invalid, would ignobly spend his time at Saratoga, when scenes like these await him in the interior of New York.

After passing many fine villages, we at last arrived at the city of Rochester. It is indeed, a large and flourishing city. It is situated on both sides of Genesee river, is well built, mostly of brick, and contains over thirteen thousand inhabitants. Near the upper part of the city, the canal crosses the river, by a splendid aqueduct of red free stone, eight hundred and four feet in length, having eleven arches, and elevated fourteen feet above the common level of the water. While the boat stopped, I went down the river to see the great falls. They are about eighty rods below where the canal crosses, and are ninety-seven feet perpendicular. Here *Sam Patch* made his last leap in the autumn of 1829. In the centre of the river, and at the verge of the precipice over which the water falls, is a ledge of rocks, called *Table Rock*, about six or seven feet in height above the water. On this Table Rock, a scaffold was erected, about twenty-five feet high, so that from the top of the scaffold to the bottom of the falls, the perpendicular height was one hundred and twenty-five feet. From this giddy height, *Sam Patch* made his "last jump," in the presence of a vast multitude of people, who had assembled to witness this daring feat, and, as it proved, fatal leap.— *Sam* never rose from the boiling flood below; but his body was carried by the current to the mouth of the river at the lake, and was there found, the next spring. Who will be the biographer of *Sam Patch?* What a pity it is some phrenologist had not examined his head.—He must have had a tremendous *jumping bump.* For myself, I could not stand on the dizzy brink of the river, and look down into the awful chasm below, with any tolerable degree of composure. These things, however, much depend upon practice. A sailor would have thought nothing of standing on the most projecting rock; or of walking along the highest precipice.

In 1811, the site of Rochester was a wilderness; now it is a large city. Its great staple of trade is flour. It contains eleven flouring mills with fifty-three run of stones; and can grind twelve thousand bushels of wheat in twenty-four hours.

After travelling from this place sixty-three miles, we found ourselves at Lockport, on the *mountain ridge.* At this place, the canal has a double row of locks adjacent to each other; five for ascending, and five for descending; each twelve feet deep, making the ascent sixty feet. This is the most admirable work of the whole canal. Between the two rows of locks, are stone steps, guarded on each side by iron railings. In 1821, there were here but two houses; now, it contains four hundred, and is a pleasant village.

Passengers for Niagara Falls, leave the canal here, as they are as near them, at this place, as they would be at Buffalo. After travelling nineteen miles, the first three of which, was through a deep cut of lime stone, from twenty to thirty feet in depth, we came in full view of the majestic Niagara river. On the margin of this stream, the canal passes by the village of Black Rock, to its termination at the city of Buffalo.

The city of Buffalo is beautifully situated on lake Erie, near its outlet; and possesses the advantages of a lake and canal navigation. It is built chiefly of brick, containing many elegant buildings, and has ten or twelve thousand inhabitants. In the harbor lay many vessels, steamboats and canal boats, and it exhibited all the show, stir and bustle of a maritime city. From this place, you have a fine view of the lake, Canada shore and the surrounding country. I was, at this time, only twenty-three miles from the celebrated *Falls of Niagara*, and I could not pass so near without going to view them.

After spending a day in Buffalo, I took a steam boat down Niagara river, to visit the Falls. On the Canada side, you have a view of the small village of Waterloo, near which, are the ruins of fort Erie, the theatre of several severe battles during the late war. On the American side, eight miles below Buffalo, is Black Rock, a pleasant village, having much romantic scenery around it. Niagara river, above the Falls, is of various breadths, from a mile and a half, to three or four miles. After passing Grand Island, I beheld the spray arising like a cloud, from the Falls; and could hear the roaring of the water. I

2

landed from the boat, about two miles above them on the American side, and took a stage. Immediately on alighting at the hotel, I walked down to the river and beheld, for the first time, the celebrated Falls of Niagara. Such a vast body of water, falling into so deep a chasm, with a noise like thunder, and with such power that it shakes the ground on which you stand, strikes one with wonder and awe! One is inclined to stand still, and gaze in silence. Other falls and deep chasms I had seen; but this presented itself on such a gigantic scale, and so much out of proportion to other objects of the kind, that it appeared to my unpractised eye incomprehensible.— Other and abler pens have given the world many minute descriptions of these Falls; and were it otherwise, I have not the vanity to suppose, any description I could give would enable any one to form a full and just conception of them.

Nature has here laid out her work upon a large scale, and with a master hand. A mighty river, the outpourings of the great lakes above, tumbling rapidly along for a mile over its rocky bed, here leaps quietly down 160 feet into the awful chasm below. Above the Falls, the banks slope gently down to the water's edge; so that you can stand on the brink of the precipice, and put your foot into the water where it rolls over it—below, the bank immediately rises, and forms a chasm 300 feet in depth. Eight or ten rods below the Falls, is the passage down to the ferry; composed, most of the way, of enclosed wooden steps; and the remainder, of steps made in the rocky cliff. I went down these steps, crossed over in the boat, tossed to and fro by the boiling, raging flood; and liberally sprinkled with the spray of the Falls. On the Canada side, the bank is not perpendicular; so that a zigzag road has been made for passengers to travel up and down it. On this side, is the Table Rock, near the Falls; and here you have the best view of them. At this spot a flight of steps lead to the bottom; and from this point a person can go 153 feet under the sheet of water. Dresses and a guide are furnished to those who have the curiosity to enter.

On my return to the American side, I walked over the bridge to Bath Island, and from that to Goat Island. This last island contains perhaps a dozen acres, is covered with a fine growth of wood, has a walk near the water, all around it, and benches and summer house to rest the weary traveller. It divides the Falls, and is probably twenty rods wide on the cliff, over which the water pitches. At the foot of this island, a circular enclosed stairway has been built by N. Biddle, Esq. President of the U. S. Bank, by which a person can descend down the cliff, between the two sheets of water. And here it was that Sam Patch leaped 118 feet from a platform, made by ladders. The trees on the island are covered with names; and the register at the hotel not only contains names, but sentiments also. I spent an evening very pleasantly in conning them over.

On the Canada side there are one large hotel and some few dwelling houses; on the American side, are two large hotels, and a fine village, called Manchester. After spending two days at the Falls, I took a seat in the stage for Buffalo.

New-York, I believe, possesses more of the sublime and beautiful, than all the remainder of the United States. It has its mountains, lakes, springs, rivers, waterfalls, canals, railroads and edifices.— Other States can show some of these, in a greater or less degree; but as a whole, New-York must bear the palm. Its resources are vast—it is a nation of itself. But notwithstanding its attractive scenery, and rich lands, the "western fever" rages here as violent as on the sterile hills of New-Hampshire.— I found more families from New-York at the West and moving thither, than from all the New-England States. They, too, seek a better country; and some would undoubtedly be discontented if they lived in paradise.

At Detroit, I saw a man who told me he had just made a purchase of a tract of land near Pontiac, about sixty miles distant in a northwest direction. He lived near Rochester, had a fine farm, raised from five hundred to one thousand bushels of wheat a year; a ready market and the average price one dollar a bushel; clear of debt, and growing rich; but the lands were cheap at the West, so he sold his farm, and was moving into the wilderness! The man was about sixty years of age; so if he has good

luck, by the time he gets a farm well cleared, a good
house and improvements, he will be too old to enjoy
earthly possessions.   But just the same feeling is
manifested in Kentucky, Ohio and Indiana.   And
even in Illinois itself, some, I found, seeking a better
country farther West!

Persons travelling to Illinois, or farther west, can
take passage in a vessel or steamboat from Buffalo
to Chicago.   The distance by water is one thousand
miles ; for they must go through Lake Erie, St.
Clair, Huron and Lake Michigan.   The distance by
land is not so far by one half ; but the water passage
is the cheapest, attended with less hardship, and
much the best way to convey goods.   There are two
other routes to Chicago.   Take a steamboat at Buffalo for Monroe, in Michigan Territory ; and from
thence, there is a good stage route, through Tecumseh, Niles, Michigan city, and along the south end
of the Lake Michigan to Chicago—or take a steamboat to Detroit ; from thence the stage to the mouth
of St. Joseph, and cross the lake in a schooner to
Chicago.   My object was to see something of Michigan ; so I took passage in a steamboat for Detroit.

On board this boat, there were probably two hundred passengers ; besides a number of horses and
oxen, wagons, household furniture and baggage.—
Most of them were emigrants, chiefly destined to
some part of Michigan.   The cabin passage is eight
dollars—deck three dollars.   Of the whole number
not more than ten took the cabin passage.   We

2*

stopped at Portland, Erie, Ashtabula, Fairport, Cleaveland and Sandusky, and arrived at Detroit in two days—distance 305 miles.

Cleaveland is the most important place on the south shore of Lake Erie. The Ohio canal here enters the lake, so that a person can go down this canal into the Ohio river; and from thence take steamboat conveyance to the western States. It is quite a large town; containing five thousand inhabitants, and has three spacious houses for public worship, a seaman's chapel, and two banks. There are three newspapers published here, and it shows all the stir and bustle of business and trade. This place has rapidly increased within a few years; and if it continues to improve in the same ratio, it will soon take its station alongside of Buffalo and Cincinnati. Its inhabitants are very spirited and enterprising.— They have contributed, as I am informed, $15,000 for the purpose of levelling down some of the high bluffs between the village and harbor, and grading the streets.

The flood of emigration, constantly pouring onward, to the far West, is immense. In the year 1833, about sixty thousand emigrants left Buffalo, to go to the West by water; and in 1834, not less than eighty thousand there embarked, besides those who took passage from other ports. No calculation can be made, of the number that have passed along the south shore of the Lake, by land; but, I was informed, a gentleman counted 250 wagons in one day!

The western world is all alive. The lakes, the streams, the prairies, and forests, are all teeming with life, and exhibit all the noise and bustle of human industry and enterprise. In 1825 there were but one steamboat and a few small schooners on Lake Erie; now there are 34 steamboats, and 150 schooners and two large brigs! And the birds and beasts of the forest are continually alarmed at the sight of human habitations and villages, so suddenly arising, within their own exclusive haunts and pleasure grounds! Monroe, in Michigan, is pleasantly situated on the river Raisin, opposite to Frenchtown, and is six miles from its mouth. It is forty miles by water, south of Detroit, and is the county seat for Monroe county, has a court house, jail, land office, three hotels, twenty-six stores, and probably two thousand inhabitants. It is situated in a fertile district, and has a number of mills and distilleries in its vicinity. A beautiful large steamboat, called the Monroe, was built here, the past season, and made its first trip down the Lake while I was at Buffalo. As this town is nearer on a direct line from Buffalo to the West than Detroit, it will shortly become the great thoroughfare of travel to the western country.

A new town has recently been laid out, on the north bank of the Maumee river. It takes the name of the river; and is situated on a plat of table land, elevated forty feet above the stream, at the foot of the falls, and ten miles from Lake Erie. The river is deep and navigable for all vessels sailing on the

Lake. The falls are about thirty feet, and afford an immense water power—equal to that of Lowell. It has now fifty dwelling houses, three stores, one tavern, a saw and grist mill; and preparations are making, to erect a large number of buildings the ensuing season; among which are four taverns. Two doctors are already settled here; and a limb of the law was on the track to join them. A glance at the map will at once show its favorable location, for a large and flourishing town. The Wabash and Erie canal, and the Cincinnati, Dayton and Erie canal, will both terminate at this place. It is situated in the disputed territory, claimed by both Ohio and Michigan; but if it should prove to be healthy, it will soon take rank with Cleaveland and Detroit. It is thirty miles south of Monroe; and about the same distance west of Lower Sandusky. A large steamboat is now building here, to run on the Lake.

On the opposite side of the river, and about a mile above, is the village of Perrysburg, of a hundred houses and twelve stores; but as its site is low, and on the shoal side of the river, its location is not therefore so favorable as that of Maumee. There are large tracts of flat land, both to the east and west of this place, covered with a heavy growth of timber.

Detroit is on the river, 25 miles above Lake Erie, and 7 below Lake St. Clair. The river is about a mile wide, and the current sets down at the rate of from two to three miles an hour. It contains about three thousand inhabitants; many of whom are French and some negroes and Indians. Much business is done here; and it will probably be one of the most important frontier towns; as it possesses a safe harbor and steamboat navigation to Buffalo, Michilimackinac, Green Bay, Chicago, &c. It is well laid out, and has some fine streets and buildings. Its public buildings are a court house, jail, academy, council house, two banks; a Presbyterian, Episcopalian, Methodist, Baptist and Catholic Churches; arsenal, magazine and commissary store house.

The streets near the water are dirty, generally having mean buildings, rather too many grog shops among them, and a good deal too much noise and dissipation. The taverns are not generally under the best regulations, although they were crowded to overflowing. I stopped at the steamboat hotel, and I thought enough grog was sold at that bar, to satisfy any reasonable demand for the whole village.— When the bell rang for dinner, I hardly knew what it meant. All in and about the house jumped and run as if the house had been on fire; and I thought that to have been the case. I followed the multitude, and found they were only going into the hall to dinner. It was a rough and tumble game at knife and fork—and whoever got seated first, and obtained the best portion of dinner, was the best fellow. Those who came after must take care of themselves the best way they could; and were not always able to obtain a very abundant supply.

At night, I was obliged to sleep in a small room having three beds in it, take a companion, and a dirty bed. In travelling, I am always disposed to make the best of every thing, and complain of nothing if it can be avoided. And in starting on this journey, I was aware, that I might suffer some hardships and inconveniences; and I had determined to bear with patience everything that was bearable; but I had not expected to be put to the test in the old settled town of Detroit. The house is large enough, and servants enough, but there was a plentiful lack of decent accommodations, in and about it.

The upper streets make a fine appearance, and are pleasant and ornamented with some elegant buildings.

Two steam ferry boats ply constantly between this, and a small village called Sandwich, on the Canada side of the river. On a pleasant afternoon, I crossed the river, and walked three or four miles on the pleasant Canada shore. From this position, Detroit shows to advantage.

Detroit has suffered much by disease. Fevers, ague and cholera, swept off its hundreds. But it is difficult to discover any other cause for the great number of deaths, than the filthiness of the place, and the dissipation and exposure of many of its inhabitants. It needs reform; and I was informed that the subject had arrested the attention of its best citizens, and they had commenced the work in good earnest.

After spending two days at Detroit, I took the stage for the mouth of St. Joseph river, on Lake Michigan—fare $9,50. The old road leads down the river, five or six miles, and then inclines to the right into the interior. The first forty miles is a level, heavily timbered country; a deep, clayey soil, and a most execrable road. Sometimes the coach became fast stuck in the deep sloughs; and we had to get out the best way we could, and help dig it out. At others, we found logs laid across the road for some distance, and the coach jolted so violently over them, that it was impossible to keep our seat. We started early in the morning from Detroit, and at ten miles stopped at a decent hotel to breakfast. It was a framed house, and of sufficient size for a common country tavern.

In this day's travel, we found some good dwellings, and one brick hotel. Late at night, " wearied and worn," we arrived at Ann Arbour, a flourishing little village on Huron river, which empties into the head of Lake Erie, and is a large, clear mill stream. The tavern house is a large three story building, finished and painted. A long block of buildings for stores, a number of mills on the stream, and a few other buildings, complete the village.

In the morning we crossed the river, on a very good bridge, and half a mile further, entered the upper village of Ann Arbour, much larger than the lower one; having two taverns, a number of stores, dwelling houses, and a court house. It is the seat of justice for Washtenaw county. Ten miles below this, on the Huron river, is situated Upsilanti, a pleasant village. The turnpike road from Detroit to Chicago passes through it; on which a stage runs, carrying the U. S. mail.

Soon after leaving this village, we came to the "oak openings." There are three kinds of land in the western country—prairie land, entirely destitute of timber and covered with grass; oak openings, land thinly covered with timber, like a northern apple orchard; and the timber land, having a dense forest of trees. All these diversities of appearance, we found from Detroit to the mouth of the St. Joseph; although the bur and white oak openings seemed to predominate.

Michigan is a level country; there are no mountains in it. It is gently undulating, for the most part; sometimes, too level and wet. It is abundantly watered and timbered, and a great deal of excellent timber. I wish I could say as much of the quality of the water. The rivers, little lakes, (and there are many of them,) streams, springs and wells, contain clear, pellucid, transparent water. It is, indeed, too clear to be agreeable to the eye; but it is all impregnated with lime, or iron, or copperas, or something disagreeable to the taste; and is in many places, very unhealthy. I do believe there is not a drop of pure, soft water, in all Michigan. I saw none, and could hear of none; and I made much inquiry, examined every river, lake, or spring, that I passed, and the result was, I found no pure water that would wash with soap, or was pleasant to the palate.

It contains much good land, many pleasant villages, fine situations, and is settling fast; but I cannot say that it is, generally, healthy.

It is probable, earth does not afford more rich and beautiful prairies than are found on the route from Monroe to Michigan city. And there are fine cultivated farms, mills and villages, and scattered settlements, all along the southern part of the territory. But I did not find the ruddy face and vigorous step of the East. The meagre and pale visage, and shaking frame, spoke a language not to be mistaken.

We passed Jackson, the seat of justice for Jackson county, near Grand river, and Marshall, the seat of justice for Calhoun county, on the bank of the Kalamazoo river, both flourishing villages. In this section of the country, mill seats are plenty, and there is an abundant supply of timber.

At the outlet of Gull Lake, I saw a well built mill, on as fine a privilege as any one could desire. At the Lake, there was a dam, which raised the water four or five feet, and made an abundant supply in the driest season—and fifty rods below where the mill was erected, there was a good fall of water.

Soon after leaving this mill, we came to Gull Prairie. This was the first prairie of much extent that I had seen; and its elegant appearance afforded me not a little pleasure. On this prairie there is a

3

small village, and a beautiful prospect around it.

The roads had become so bad, that we left the stage coach, after two days' ride, and took a wagon, without any spring seats; and I found it so fatiguing to ride, that I often preferred walking. When we arrived at this little village, it was late in the evening, but we had still twelve miles to go that night.

It was past midnight when we crossed the Kalamazoo river, at the rope ferry, and entered the town of Bronson. This is the seat of justice, or as the term is here, county seat, for Kalamazoo county. The land office, for the southern part of the territory, is also kept here. We found a large tavern house and good accommodations, a pleasant village, and pleasant people.

Our route now lay through an undulating, open country for twenty miles, when we came to a house and mill on Pawpaw river; where we " ate our breakfast for our dinner." We now crossed the stream, and travelled a new road, generally through timbered land, passed seven or eight small lakes, for 28 miles, before we came to a house.

Here, we found two log houses adjoining each other. It had now become night, and at this place we were to stay till the next day. I went in, and asked the woman, if she could get us something to eat. She said, if we would accept of such fare as she had, she would try. When we went in to supper, I never was more agreeably surprised in my life. We found a table neatly set; and upon it,

venison steaks, good warm wheat bread, good butter, wild honey in the white comb, and a good cup
of tea—better fare than we had found in Michigan,
and as good as could be obtained anywhere. Our
accommodations at this log house in the woods,
show what people may do if they choose. And I
wish some tavern keepers of our large towns, might
happen to call there, and learn a lesson which they
seem too much disinclined to learn at home. Our
bill was so moderate, we added a dollar to it, and
hardly thought we had fully paid our hostess then.

Twelve miles further, brought us to the river St.
Joseph, about a mile above where it empties into
the Lake. The river here is thirty rods wide. We
crossed it in a ferry boat, and after ascending a high
bluff, we came in full view of Lake Michigan and
the St. Joseph village.

This village is pleasantly situated on a high bluff,
on the south side of the river, and facing the Lake ;
and contains sixty or seventy houses, two taverns,
some half dozen stores, two large warehouses, and a
light house. One tavern, the stores, and a few
dwelling houses, are built underneath the bluff, on
the bank of the river. A steamboat plies between
this place and Niles, fifty miles up the river, as it
runs, but only 25 miles by land. Just above the
village, is a steam saw mill, which does a good deal
of business. This place carries on considerable
trade with the interior ; the staple of which is
wheat.

St. Joseph is very unhealthy.   At the tavern, I
found three persons sick, and one dangerously so.
I called upon the doctor, and he was sick abed ; I
called upon the baker, and he was sick abed—and
I passed by another house, where the whole family,
consisting of a man, his wife, and five children, were
all sick abed, and so completely helpless, that the
neighbors had to take care of them! This is no
fiction.   The man's name is Emerson; from the
State of New-York.   Last spring, he came on to
this part of the country with his family and goods in
a wagon.   And when he came to Pawpaw river,
where we breakfasted, he found no road direct to
St. Joseph.   He accordingly cut out the road that
we had travelled to this place, and was the first who
came through with a wagon, a distance of about
fifty miles.   Soon after his arrival, his eldest son, a
promising youth of fifteen, accidentally was drowned in the river.   The family, one by one, were taken
sick ; and now, all were sick and helpless.   The
man possessed great vigor of mind and body ; had
bought him a farm at some distance from the village
on the road he had made, and commenced some
improvements, and made great efforts to persevere
and clear it up.   But who can withstand the iron
grasp of disease, or the " bold demands of death !"
He beheld his family wasting away and to all appearance, hastening to the grave ; and himself, as
sick and helpless as they.   A sad catastrophe this,
in his prospect of wealth and bliss in the new world !

A schooner, called the Philip, plies regularly between this, and Chicago across the Lake ; but I had to wait here three days before its return. I spent the time in traversing the woods and the lake shore. This Lake is a clear, beautiful sheet of water, having a soft sandy shore, and surrounded by high sandy hills. The river makes a good harbor, but there is a sand bar at its mouth, on which there is not more than five or six feet of water. The average width of the Lake is sixty miles.

The distance from Detroit to St. Joseph is two hundred miles, and we had been five days and a half in travelling it. The road was as good as could be expected in a country so new, and so thinly inhabited. The land generally is good, and will support a dense population. The southern part of the territory is thought to contain the best land, and there are indeed some beautiful prairies. Prairie Round is among the most beautiful. It contains a number of hundred acres of high, level, and smooth land ; and in the centre, there is a dozen acres of higher land, covered with a beautiful growth of trees.

The best part of Indiana is on the border of Michigan, and extending south, on the Wabash river. The southern part of the State contains a good deal of hilly, rocky and sandy land, unfit for cultivation.

A territorial road has been laid out from Detroit to St. Joseph ; and a survey of a railroad has been

3*

made, nearly on the line of the road, between the
two places; but sometime will elapse, before either
are completed.

Wild game is plenty; deer, ducks, bears, wolves
and squirrels are in sufficient quantity to keep the
hunter awake.

Upon the whole, if good water and good health
could be found, Michigan would be a very desirable
country in which to reside.

As soon as the vessel was ready to depart, I took
passage in her. We sailed round the south end of
the Lake, and stopped at Michigan city, a village of
twenty or thirty houses, and twelve stores, situated
on the corner of Indiana, among the sand hills of
the Lake. A small stream here empties into the
Lake but affords no harbor for vessels. Some enterprising citizens have determined to make it a
large town; but nature does not seem much to have
seconded their efforts. It is forty miles from St.
Joseph, and just the same distance from Chicago.
The stage road, from Michigan city to Chicago, is,
most of the way, on the sandy beach.

Chicago makes a fine appearance when viewed
from the water. It has a light house, fort and barracks in which a garrison is kept, and many elegant
buildings. It is regularly laid out, on the south side
of Chicago river; the streets running parallel with
it, and others crossing them at right angles. The
harbor being too much exposed, a breakwater is
building, so as to render it secure and safe for the

shipping. The town is already compactly built, for more than a mile in length, and about half that distance in width; and there are a dozen houses on the north side of the river, with which it is connected by an elegant bridge. It has thirty-six stores some of which are large and elegant, and built of brick; and seven large taverns, filled with guests to overflowing. It is now, about the size of Exeter, in New-Hampshire, and is rapidly increasing. Vessels and steamboats come here from Buffalo, laden with goods and merchandize; and it is the great thoroughfare for travel to the western country. The trade of all the upper country centres here; and when the canal is completed, connecting the Lake with the waters of the Illinois river, it must become the largest town in the State. It is built on a level prairie, open in full view to the Lake, and the soil is enough mixed with sand, to prevent its being muddy. The Lake supplies the town with good, wholesome water, and as far as I could judge, it is quite healthy.

While I was at Chicago, the Pottawattomie tribe of Indians, came there to receive their annuity from the United States government. I could not accurately ascertain their number, but probably, there were between two and three thousand, men, women and children. I had before seen the small remnants of Indian tribes at the north; but never had I seen such a large body of western Indians assembled together. I had much curiosity to see them, and

learn something of the Indian character.   In this I
was fully gratified.

Those who have formed high notions of the state-
liness and chivalry of the Indian character, might
gain some new ideas, by witnessing, day after day,
the actions and movements of the Pottawattomies.
It is painful to state it, but truth compels me to say,
their appearance was, with but few exceptions, that
of a drunken set of miserable vagabonds.   They
were generally mounted on horseback, men, women
and children ; some had small bells for their horses—
some had blankets on, and others had coats and pan-
taloons, similar to the whites ; and many of them,
had jewels in the nose and ears, and the face painted in various colors and forms, so as to give them
either a ludicrous, or terrific appearance.

To all this, perhaps, no one has a right seriously
to object.   It is merely a matter of taste ; and if
they choose to exhibit themselves in the various hues
of the rainbow, or in the terrific aspect of a warrior,
I am willing they should be gratified.   But their
actions were beneath the dignity of man, or of beast.
They encamped near the town, on the border of the
lake ; and above it, on the margin of the river.   I
walked all through their encampment, and saw them
frequently in the streets.   I found them, generally,
bickering, quarelling, or fighting ; or running their
horses through the town, and displaying all the antics
of madmen.   Day after day, and night after night,
they were carousing, shouting and fighting.   On

the lake shore, one of them killed his wife, by splitting her head open with a hatchet, and then fled! I did not learn what became of him.

They are also much addicted to theft. Too lazy to work, they had rather steal whatever they desire, that comes in their way; and this propensity and practice has been a fruitful source of the border wars, between the whites and Indians.

I have seen hundreds of negroes together on their holidays; when they had free access to intoxicating liquor if they chose; when they gave themselves up to pastime and pleasure; and I do say, they appeared much more civil and decent to themselves and to others, than the Indians. They did not seem, like the Indians, to lose *all* self respect.— The negroes generally appear to possess amiable dispositions; and are faithful friends; are much more pliant and teachable; and if I must dwell with either negroes or Indians, give me the negroes.

If the former mode of paying the government annuity to the chief of a tribe, were objectionable, the present mode of paying each individual, seems to me to be equally, if not more objectionable. I was informed that the gross sum of seventy thousand dollars was paid to them individually; each one an equal portion of that amount. But after spending a few days in carousing at Chicago, they left the town, as they will finally leave the world, carrying nothing with them!

It appears to me, some different regulations, respecting the Indians, ought to be adopted. The money now paid them, upon the whole, seems to do them more hurt than good. Might not the government pay them in specific articles, instead of money, such as blankets, clothing, implements of husbandry, &c. There would not be then quite so much inducement for speculators to prey upon them.

As to civilization, I am not so sanguine as some are, that it can be done. The Indians seem to be naturally averse to the restraints and labor of civilized life. To beg or steal is much more agreeable to them, than to labor for subsistence. Anything that looks like work, they despise. In all cases, where they have come in contact with the whites, it has been death to the Indian. At the approach of civilization, they wither away and die ; and the remnants of tribes must flee away to the fastnesses of the wilderness, or perish in the withering grasp of civilized man. They are to be pitied ; but their unprovoked murders and savage cruelties, have steeled the heart against them. Their cold-blooded murders, in the late war in Illinois, of men, women and children, and their indecent mutilation and exposure of their bodies when dead, cannot soon be forgotten or forgiven. Black Hawk, the cold-blooded instigator and leader in this war, dared not return from his trip to the East through Chicago, and the theatre of his cruelties, He probably will never again set his foot on the eastern shore of the Mississippi.

The country back of Chicago, for the distance of twelve miles, is a smooth, level prairie ; producing an abundance of grass, but too low and wet for cultivation. The Chicago river is formed by two branches, which meet at the upper end of the village. The branches come from exactly opposite directions, and after running some distance, parallel with the lake, and about a mile from it, here meet each other, and turning at right angles, flow in a regular straight channel, like a canal, into the lake. On each side of the town, between these branches and the lake shore, there is, for some distance, a good growth of wood and timber. On the lake shore, there are naked sand hills ; and these are found all around the lake.

This world has undergone great changes since its original creation. In examining the western country, I came to the conclusion, that a large portion of it was once under water ; and that the lakes formerly discharged their waters into the sea, through the Illinois and Mississippi rivers.

The lakes Michigan, Huron, St. Clair and Erie, are now about twenty-five feet lower than Lake Superior. The Falls of St. Mary, at the outlet of the upper lake, are nothing more than rapids. The water descends twenty-two feet in the distance of three quarters of a mile ; and although canoes can pass them either way, yet they are impassable to steamboats and vessels. Some years ago, a large

vessel did go down them in safety.   It was built on
Lake Superior, by the North-western Fur Company,
but was found to be too large to be useful in their
trade.   It was taken to the Falls of St. Mary, and
some Indians were hired to take it down the rapids.
They happened to go down in safety ; and the vessel was afterwards sold at Buffalo.   Now, the pro-
bability is, that these lower lakes were once nearly
on a level with Lake Superior ; and their outlet was
at the south end of Lake Michigan, instead of the
Niagara river.

Eight or ten miles from the present limits of Lake
Erie, there is a regular, well defined shore, once
washed by the water; plainly indicating that the
lake was once about twenty feet higher than it now
is. If Lake Michigan were ten feet higher than its
present level, its waters would flow into the Illinois
river.   The Oplanes, a branch of the Illinois, approaches within twelve miles of the Lake ; and the
land between is low and level.   When the water is
high, boats now pass from the lake to the river.   At
a time of high water, a steamboat attempted to pass
from the Illinois to the lake.   After running a day
from Ottawa up the river, the water began to subside,
the captain became alarmed, lest his boat might run
aground and returned.

The valley of the Illinois river, plainly indicates
that a much larger stream once run there.   Had its
channel been formed by its present quantity of water,
it would have been not more than forty rods wide ;

but now, it carries a breadth of from fifty rods to more than a mile; it is, therefore, full of shoals and sand bars. The high banks all along down the stream, are about two miles apart; and the space between them not occupied by the river, is either a low marsh or a narrow lake.

When the lakes were high, aided probably by a strong west wind, the water broke through in the direction of Niagara river; and in process of time, wore a deep channel, drained the lakes to their present level, and dried up their outlet, at the south end of Lake Michigan. This is my theory; and whoever will examine the country around the lakes, may not deem it as wild and extravagant a one, as has been advanced and believed by mankind.

Many of the inhabitants of Chicago are from the eastern part of the country—civil, enterprising and active. I found good society here—much better than I had expected in a place so new, and of such rapid growth. But there is one house here, that is a public nuisance; and which travellers would do well to avoid. It professes to be a tavern; has assumed the name of the "Tremont House;" but is in fact a gambling house of the worst character. It is the universal resort of the gamblers, the dissipated and disorderly; and the inhabitants were often disturbed at midnight by their shouts and contentions. But such a disorderly house cannot long be suffered to exist. A prosecution was commenced against its keeper, and a number of its inmates arrested, while

4

I was there.   And the authorities of the place were
determined to break it up entirely.

House rent here is high, and provisions are dear.
Last spring, potatoes were sold for a dollar and a
half a bushel ; and this fall the current price is a dollar.   All this is owing to the rapid increase of the
place, and the immense travel through it.   When
more houses are built, and the country back of it
becomes settled, living will, undoubtedly, be cheap.
To the man of enterprise and business, it affords as
good a location as any in the western country.

At this place I found three young men from New-
England, who were travelling to see the western
country.   We hired two horses and a wagon, at
seventy-five cents a day, and started together into
the interior of Illinois, west of Chicago.

It was past the middle of October; the air was
mild and clear, and the earth dry.   The prairie,
which in the spring of the year is so wet and muddy
as to be difficult to pass, we found dry, and a good
smooth road over it; so we travelled merrily on.   At
the distance of twelve miles the ground became
elevated a few feet, and we found a fine grove of
timber, a few log houses, and the Oplanes river.   At
this place the roads fork—one goes south, to Ottawa
on the Illinois river—the other goes in a westerly
direction, to Galena on the Mississippi.   Stages run
from Chicago, over each of these roads to both
places, carrying the U. S. mail.

The roads in this country are in a state of nature. But the ground is so smooth, and so entirely free from stones, that when the earth is dry you do not find better roads at the north. Indeed, you can travel in a carriage over most part of the country, woods and all.

We took the Galena road, forded the river, a stream about four rods wide, and passed on, over a beautiful, open, prairie country, here and there a log house, a small grove of timber, or small stream of water; the land high, dry and rich, and arrived at night at Naper's settlement, on the Du Page river, thirty-seven miles from Chicago. Naper was the first settler here. He keeps a public house, very decent accommodations; has a store and mills, and is forming a village around him. Here is a large grove of good timber.

We now left the Galena road and took a course more northerly to the *big* and *little woods*, on Fox river. In travelling twelve miles we came to the settlement, at the lower end of " little woods." In the space of three miles, we found about twenty families, all in comfortable log houses; fields fenced and cultivated ; a school house erecting, and a master hired to keep two months. And among the whole, only one family had been there two years; the remainder had none of them been there quite a year. The houses were built near the timber, and a beautiful rich prairie opened before them.

The man who had been here two years had a hundred acres under fence; raised a large crop of corn and wheat, and had sold at Chicago, only thirty miles distant in a straight line, two hundred and twenty bushels of potatoes for as many dollars. He had built a wear across the river to catch fish, which I walked down to see. He took his boat, went out to the pen, and dipped out with a small net half a boat load of fish.

This is a land of plenty sure enough; and if a man cannot here obtain the luxuries of the city, he can obtain all the necessaries of life in abundance.

Fox river is a clear stream of water, about twenty rods wide, having a hard limestone bottom, from two to three feet deep, a brisk current, and generally fordable. On its banks, and on some other streams, we occasionally found ledges of limestone ; but other than that, we found no rocks in the State.

We here forded the river, and travelled all day on its western bank. We found less timber on this side of the river. On the east side, it is generally lined with timber to the depth of a mile or more; but the west side is scarcely skirted with it. It is somewhat singular and unaccountable, but we found it universally to be the fact, that the east side of all the streams had much the largest portion of timber.

We passed a number of log houses, all of which had been built the present season, and came at last to the upper house on the river. The man told us,

he had been here with his family only three days.—
In attempting to get at the head of population, we
more than once thought of the story of the Ohio
pumpkin vine; and concluded if we accomplished
it, we should be obliged to run our horses. He
said, in the morning his was the upper house on the
river; but a man had made a location above him,
and perhaps had already built him a house.

We went a few miles above this, forded the river,
passed through the woods into the open prairie, and
started down the east side. We travelled on, until
it became dark. We were in an open prairie, without any road, a cloudy night, and had no means of
directing our course. It was a great oversight, but
we had no fire works with us, and the wolves began
to howl around at a distance. We concluded we
should be obliged to stay out that night, and without any fire. A man accustomed to the new country, would probably have thought nothing of it; but
to me, who had never lodged out doors in my life,
to be obliged to camp out in a new country, and
among the wolves, and such other wild animals as
chose to come along, it was not quite so pleasant. I
confess I began to have some misgivings in my own
mind, whether this new world ought, in fact, to be
called a paradise.

We knew that if there were any houses in that
region, they would be near the woods; we accordingly obliqued to the right, and after some time travelling saw a light, which led us to a house.

4*

These log houses generally have one large room, in which the family cook, eat and lodge ; and if any strangers come, they lodge in the same room with the family, either in a bed or on the floor, as may be the most convenient. They are built of logs locked together at the corners; the interstices filled with timber split like rails, and plastered over with clay. The roofs are covered with shingles about four feet long; the chimnies are built on the outside, with wood, and lined with clay ; and the floor is made of split timber. Many of them are quite neat and warm.

The next day we passed a few miles down the river, crossed it, and travelled twenty or thirty miles west, towards Rock river. Our whole course lay through an open prairie. We could see timber on either hand. This day we found a number of gravel hills, the tops of which were coarse, naked gravel, and looked white at a distance. They were from ten to twenty feet high. We walked up to the top of the highest one, and had an extended view of the surrounding country. From this elevation we could see the timber on the border of Rock river.

We obliqued more to the south, came to a grove of timber and a house. Here we stayed that night. The next day we took a southeasterly direction, passed one house, and came to Fox river, where the Galena road crosses it. We forded the river, and travelling over an open rolling prairie twenty miles in a southeasterly direction, came to Walker's grove.

on the Du Page river, forty miles south of Chicago.
Here we found a tavern, saw and grist mill, and
something of a village, having two or three framed
houses among the log huts.

The U. S. mail stage passes from Chicago through
this place, Ottawa, Peoria and Springfield to St.
Louis; and agreeably to our previous arrangement,
I here left my companions, who returned to Chicago; and I took the stage for the south. I had
travelled with them just long enough to be fully sen-
sible of the great loss I sustained at parting. Thus
it is with the traveller. He forms acquaintances and
finds friends; but it is only to part with them, probably forever.

Before I go into the lower part of the State, I
shall stop here, and say a few words of the appearance, present condition and future prospects of the
northern part of Illinois. I feel in some degree
qualified to do this, not only from my own observa-
tion, but from information obtained from intelligent
and respectable sources.

The northern part of Illinois is beautifully diversified with groves of timber and rolling prairies. The
timber consists of the various kinds of oak, rock
and white maple, beach, locust, walnut, mulberry,
plum, elm, bass wood, buckeye, hackberry, sycamore,
spice wood, sassafras, haws, crab apple, cherry, cucumber, papaw, &c. There is some cedar, but little pine. The shores of Michigan have a large

supply of pine timber, and from this source the lumber for buildings at Chicago is obtained.

The prairies are sometimes level, sometimes gently undulating, and sometimes hilly; but no where mountainous. The soil is three or four feet deep; then you come to a bed of clay two or three feet in depth, and then gravel. The soil is a rich, black loam; and when wet, it sticks to the feet like clay. Manure has no beneficial effect upon it; but where it has been cultivated, it produces an abundant crop, the first year not quite as good as succeeding years; and it seems to be quite inexhaustible. The prairies are covered with a luxuriant growth of native grass, which when it gets its full growth is generally about as high as a man's shoulders; they are destitute of trees, shrubs, or stones; and although the surface may be undulating, yet it is so smooth, that they can be mown as well as the smoothest old field in New-England. In the spring of the year, a great variety of beautiful flowers shoot up among the grass; so that the face of nature exhibits the appearance of an extended flower garden. The prairie grass is unlike any kind I have seen at the north; but it affords excellent fodder for horses, neat cattle and sheep. A finer grazing country I have never seen. The grass appears to have more nourishment in it, than at the north. I saw beef cattle, fatted on the prairie grass alone, and I challenge Brighton to produce fatter beef, or finer flavored.

Towards the lake, the land is gently undulating ; farther west, on Fox and Rock rivers, it is rolling; and as you approach Galena on the Mississippi, it becomes more hilly and broken. All this country seems to lack, is timber and water. There are rivers enough, but not many small streams and springs. But both of these defects can in a good measure be remedied. Good water can be obtained almost anywhere by digging wells from twenty to thirty feet in depth ; and fuel must be supplied by the coal, which is found generally in abundance throughout the State. Bricks can be used for building; and hedge rows for fences. The coal is excellent for the grate. It burns free, and emits such a brilliant light, that any other in a room is hardly necessary. It is now used in many places, in preference to wood, although that is now plenty. Blacksmiths use it for the forge; and at one shop, the man told me he could dig and haul enough in half a day to last him a month.

The government of the United States granted to the State of Illinois a tract of land ten miles in width and eighty miles in length, extending from Chicago to Ottawa, for the purpose of making a canal to connect the waters of the lake with the Illinois river, and within these limits it is supposed the canal will pass. This tract has been surveyed, put into market and much of it sold; but most of the land in the northern part of the State had not even been surveyed when I was there. Not a survey had

been made on Fox river.   The settlers took as much
land as they pleased, and where they pleased ; and
as there was an abundance for all, none found fault.
Before this time, I presume, the land has been surveyed ;   and the peace and quietness of the Fox
river settlement, may have been a little disturbed by
the *carelessness* of the United States surveyors, in
running lines somewhat diverging from the stakes
and fences which its early settlers had set up as the
bounds of their farms.

But a large portion of the northern half of the
State, is not in the market, and perhaps may not be
for two years to come.   This very land, however, is
settling every day.   All a man has to do, is to select
his land, and settle down upon it.   By this act he
gains a *pre-emption right* to one hundred and sixty
acres ;   and before the auction sale, enters his land at
the land office, pays a dollar and a quarter an acre,
and receives his title.   When land has once been
through the auction and not sold, it can be taken at
any time, by paying a dollar and a quarter an acre,
and receive a title.

Upon the whole, I think the upper part of Illinois
offers the greatest inducements to the emigrant, especially from the northern States.   It is a high,
healthy, beautiful country ; and there are now plenty
of good locations to be made.   A young man, with
nothing but his hands to work, may in a few years
obtain a competency.   The whole country produces
great crops of wheat, corn and potatoes, and all the

fruits and vegetables of the north. Apple and peach trees grow faster and more vigorous here than at the east; and there is a native plum tree, which bears excellent fruit.

I took much pains to ascertain whether it was subject to the fever and ague; and from the inquiries I made, and the healthy appearance of the people, I am persuaded it is not. I found only one person sick with that disease, in all the upper country, and she was an old woman from Indiana; and she told me she had it before she left that State.— There is plenty of game—the prairie hen, about the size of the northern hen, deer, ducks, wild turkies, and squirrels; also an abundance of wild honey.

There is another reason why the northern part of the State is preferable. Chicago of itself is, and will be, something of a market for produce; but it is the best spot in the whole State, to carry produce to be transported to a northern market. From this it is carried all the way by water to New-York city; and the distance is no greater than from the middle and lower parts of the State to New-Orleans, and the expense of transportation the same.

But after all, there is no such place as a perfect elysium on earth; and to this bright picture of the new world, there must be added some slight shades. In the first place, there are many prairie wolves all over the country, so that it is almost impossible to keep sheep. In travelling over the country, I have started half a dozen in a day; they did not appear to be very wild; but they seldom, or never attack a man, unless retreat is cut off, or sorely pressed by hunger. They are of a brown color, and of the size of a large dog. The men have a good deal of sport in running them down, and killing them.— They take a stick, mount a fleet horse, soon come up with them, and knock them on the head.

A man on Fox river told me he made a wolf pen over a cow that got accidentally killed, and caught twelve wolves in one week! As the country becomes settled they will disappear. There are but few bears; the country is too open for them. I had one or two meals of bear meat, but it is not at all to my taste. Then, there is the prairie rattlesnake, about a foot long. Their bite is not considered very dangerous. There is a weed, growing universally on the prairie, that is a certain cure for it. They are not, however, plenty. Men told me, that they had passed a whole year without seeing one.

Then, to prey upon the fields of the husbandman, there are the blackbirds and squirrels. They are the same in kind with those of the north, and their rapacity seems to have lost nothing, by living at the west. The blackbird is not a bird of the forest; it only follows close upon the heels of population.

The winters are as cold, perhaps, as at the north, but of shorter duration. They commence later and end earlier. The Indians make their ponies get their living in the winter; and cattle will live if they can have a range in the woods; but the·farmer can have as much hay as he chooses, only for the cutting; the good husbandman will, therefore, have enough to keep his cattle in good heart during the winter.

Men are apt to judge of a new country by the impulse of feeling. The enthusiastic admirer of nature, when he beholds the extended prairies, lofty groves and pellucid streams, represents it as a perfect paradise. But those who think more of good roads, good coaches, good houses and good eating, than they do of the beauties of nature, curse the whole country and quit it in disgust. But to prevent all mistakes, be it known to all whom it may concern, that in this new country, fields do not grow ready fenced and planted, and elegant houses beside them ; pancakes are not found on trees, or roasted pigs, running about squealing to be eaten.

The jaundiced eye sees nothing in its true light.

> ———— " The diff'rence is as great between
> " The optics seeing, as the objects seen :
> " Or fancy's beam enlarges, multiplies,
> " Contracts, inverts, and gives a thousand dyes."

Many anecdotes were told me, of the different views the same individual would have of the same place, under different circumstances. An emigrant from Vermont, with his wife, children and goods, started for the western world in a wagon. The country was new, and the roads so bad that their progress was slow and fatiguing. At length, after enduring many privations and hardships in a jour-

5

ney of twelve hundred miles, they safely arrived in
Illinois, and located themselves on a fine, rich spot
of ground, in the interior. He hastily threw up a
temporary hut for their present accommodation ; but
they were all too much wearied and worn, vigorously
to exert themselves. He became sad himself; his
wife, unable to restrain her feelings, began to sob
aloud, and the children joined the concert. They
could not divert their thoughts from the home,
neighbors and friends they had left. The prairie
and wild wood had no charms for them. After
three or four days of despondency, they picked
up their goods, loaded their wagon, and trudged all
the way back again to Vermont. Vermont had,
however, lost *some* of its charms. It did not appear quite as fine as they had expected. After
spending another cold winter there, they began to
think Illinois, upon the whole, was the better place ;
and that they had been very foolish in leaving it.—
So, they picked up their duds again, returned to the
same spot they had left, and were satisfied, contented and happy. The man has now an excellent
farm, good house, and an abundance of the necessaries and conveniences of life. In short, he is an
independent farmer, and he would not now, upon
any consideration, return to Vermont.

An instance in some respects similar to this, occurred some years ago, in an emigrant from the western
part of the State of New-Hampshire. He sold his
farm, and started for Ohio. His wife and children,

and a portion of his furniture, he put into a large
wagon, drawn by three or four yoke of oxen; and
three cows of a peculiar breed, he also took with
him. They proceeded on about five hundred miles,
probably as far as Buffalo, when they all became
weary, and so excessively fatigued with their journey, that they lost all relish for the western country,
and wished themselves back again. At this time,
they held a council, and agreed, without a dissent-
ing voice, to return to New-Hampshire. They accordingly wheeled about, cows and all, and trudged
back to the town they had left; having performed a
journey of a thousand miles with an ox-team, at
great expense, and apparently to no beneficial purpose whatever. He did not, however, like the Ver-
monter, again return.

But the result of the trip was not as disastrous as
had been anticipated. At the very time of their return, a much better farm than the one he had left
was offered for sale, for ready money. He bought
it at a reduced price, and immediately settled upon
it. He then made a calculation upon his present
and former condition; and after taking into consideration the expenses of his journey, the sale of one
farm and purchase of another, he found himself
worth at least a thousand dollars more than he was
previous to the transaction!

And here, I would give a caution to the emigrant
who intends to settle in the western country, not to
place implicit confidence in what the inhabitants of

one section may say of other portions of it.   If they
mean to be honest in giving an opinion, self interest
as in other places, strangely warps their judgment.
Land holders and actual settlers are anxious to build
up their own village and neighborhood; and therefore, they praise their own section and decry the
others.   At Detroit, we are told that Monroe is a
very sickly place; at Monroe, Detroit is unhealthy;
and both will concur that Chicago is too unhealthy
for an emigrant to think of enjoying life in it.   In
Michigan, that is the most healthy, pleasant and best
portion of the West; in Illinois, that becomes the
promised land.   Indeed, so contradictory are their
statements, that little reliance ought to be placed
upon them; and the better way for the emigrant is,
if he cannot obtain the necessary information from
disinterested travellers, to go and examine for himself.   Eastern people, who travel no farther than
Michigan, generally form an unfavorable opinion of
Chicago and Illinois; but were they to travel over
that State, they would soon change their opinion.

But I have dwelt long enough on the upper country.   I took the stage and travelled twenty-five
miles over an open prairie, passing only one house,
and arrived at night at Holderman's grove.   This is
a pleasant grove of excellent timber, having by its
side a number of good houses and large cultivated
fields.

The next morning, we rode fifteen miles to Ottawa, where we breakfasted.   Here the Illinois and

Fox rivers join, and appear to be nearly of equal size, both about twenty rods wide. The village is on the east side of the Illinois river, which we crossed in a ferry boat. A tavern, some houses and stores are built on a small flat under the hill, and a number of houses on a bluff, two hundred feet above the river. Steamboats come up as high as this place, unless the water be quite low. If it be not a sickly place, I am much mistaken. The fever and ague seems to be the prevailing disease. I have observed that situations on the western rivers are generally unhealthy.

The river diverges to the west, and the road down the country immediately leaves it. In travelling twenty-five miles, I found myself fourteen from the river. Here I left the stage, and went to Hennipen, a small village on the Illinois river. It is regularly laid out on a high, level prairie, which extends three miles back, and consists of two taverns, four stores, a dozen dwelling houses and a court house— it being the seat of justice for Putnam county. I found a number of people sick in this place with the fever and ague.

Here I crossed the river, about fifty rods wide, in a ferry boat, and found on the other side about two miles of heavy timbered bottom land, subject to overflow. From this, I ascended a high bluff, passed three or four miles of oak openings, and then came into the open prairie.

5*

Ten miles from the river, a new town, called Princeton, is laid out in the prairie, on the stage road leading from Peoria to Galena. Three buildings, one of which was a store where the Post Office is kept, had been erected when I was there; but as it is in a healthy situation, and surrounded by a beautiful rich country, it may in time become a large village.

I travelled some distance in a northerly direction, between great and little Bureau rivers. The larger stream has a number of mills upon it. The country around here, is too similar to the upper part of the State to need a particular description. High rolling prairies, skirted with timber, everywhere abound in this region, and present to the eye a most beautiful landscape. It is mostly settled by people from New-England; and they appeared healthy, contented and happy—and are in fact, becoming rich and independent farmers.

One northern man I called upon, whose past and present condition may be similar to many others. I will state it for the edification of those who live on the rocky soil of New-England. While at the north, he lived on a hilly and rocky farm; had a large family, and was obliged to work hard and use the strictest economy, to support them, and meet the current expenses of the year. Tired of severe labor and small gains, he sold his farm and moved to the State of Illinois. He had been here two years; has now one hundred acres under fence;

raised the present season fifteen hundred bushels of corn, three hundred of wheat; has seventy head of neat cattle and sixty hogs. He has a fine timber lot near his house, in which is an abundance of the sugar maple. He had killed, the present season, four beef cattle, the last one just before I called upon him; and fatter and better flavored beef I never saw. All the cattle grow exceedingly fat on the prairie grass; so much so, that corn will add nothing to it. A saw and grist mill are within seven miles of him. He was getting out timber, and intended to put up a two story house in the spring. I enquired particularly as to the health of his family and neighborhood. He informed me it had been very healthy; his own family had not any of them been sick abed a day, since they came into the country. Two of his daughters are well married, and settled on farms near him. Let every farmer at the north, who has to tug and toil on the sterile and rocky soil of New-England, to support his family, judge for himself, whether it is better to go to the West, or stay where he is. Whether, in fact, it is better to struggle for existence, and feel the cold grasp of poverty, or to roll in plenty and live at ease.

This region was somewhat the theatre of Indian cruelties in the last war with the whites. One northern man became their victim in this settlement. His name was Elijah Philips, of New-Hampshire. When he was at the age of twenty-one, he took his pack on his back, travelled to the West, and located himself in what is called the Yankee Settlement, on the Bureau river. He was a persevering, hardy son of the North. He built a house, fenced in a field, obtained some stock and a few hogs; and was in a fair way to gain a competency and become an independent farmer. Just at this time, the Indian war broke out, with the blood-thirsty Black Hawk as a leader.

Murders having been committed above them, the settlers deemed their situation insecure, and fled to the east side of the Illinois river. After remaining there awhile, the war still raging, and its termination uncertain, seven of the settlers armed themselves with guns and bayonets, took a wagon, and went to the settlement to bring away such articles of household furniture and husbandry as they could; fearing the Indians might destroy them. They spent the day in collecting their articles together. At night, they left them and the wagon where they were, and concluded to go themselves to a house half a mile below, which was deemed more secure. Here they slept quietly all night, opened the door early in the morning, looked all around, but saw no signs of Indians. Philips and another young man said they would go up to the other house and commence loading the wagon. They started off together.

In about twenty rods from the house, the path led along by a point of timber that made out into the prairie; and when they had gone about half

way to this point, the other young man stopped, returned back, and Philips passed on alone. He had
just got into the house, when he heard a piercing cry
of alarm from Philips, and in a moment after, the
report of two guns. On running to the door, he
saw Philips prostrate on the ground, and twenty or
thirty Indians leaping out of the thicket. He rallied
his companions, as they had not all yet risen, caught
two guns, handed one to a man near him, and by
the time they reached the door, the Indians were
coming round the corner of the house. On seeing
the guns with fixed bayonets, they dodged back.—
In a moment, they were all at the ends and rear of
the house, rending the air with their astounding
war cry, flourishing their tomahawks in menace and
defiance ; but took special care not to come in front
of the door. The settlers were all young men—the
onset had been so sudden and boisterous, that they
were taken entirely by surprise, and hardly knew
what they did. On a moment's reflection, they concluded, if they contended manfully, there might be
some chance for life. Although the number of Indians might be ten to one of theirs, yet they had
the advantage of being within a well built log house,
impenetrable by balls.

Spirited and prompt action saved them. While
the Indians were hovering round, in doubt what
course to take to dislodge them, they dug out a
chink between the logs in the rear, and thrust out
their guns. The moment this was done, the In-

dians changed the tone of their yells, leaped for the woods, fell flat on their faces and crawled unperceived away.

They now felt relieved from immediate danger. They knew there was a company of horse at Hennipen, fifteen miles distant; and their only safe course seemed to be, to send for them if they could. They had a horse with them, and he was feeding on the prairie about thirty rods from the house, nearly on the opposite side from the spot where the Indians entered the woods; but as they could not know where they might be, none deemed it prudent to go out to catch him. They called the horse, however, and although he was one generally hard to catch, he now started at once, came to the door, thrust in his head and stood still while the bridle was put on.—One of their number mounted, and rode express to Hennipen.

In the afternoon, the troop arrived; reconnoitered the neighborhood; found the Indian trail; followed it a number of miles; but they had gone beyond their reach. On a further examination of the woods, it was apparent, the Indians had been hovering around them all the day before while at work; but were too cowardly to attack them, although they knew the smallness of their number.

The situation of affairs at night they also knew full well. They truly supposed that *all* would pass the spot where they lay in ambush, in the morning. But accidentally, *one* passed alone, and discovered them, and was undoubtedly the cause of saving the lives of all the rest. But had the other young man passed on instead of returning, and why he did not, he never could tell, although the question was asked him immediately after the transaction, he also would have been killed; and in that event, probably all the others would have been sacrificed; for it was quite early in the morning, and they had not risen.

On examining Philips, they discovered that two musket balls had entered his body—one in the region of the heart, so that he must have died immediately. His remains were carried to Hennipen for interment; and when I passed that way, I stopped at his grave to show, what I felt, respect to his memory. On a small eminence in the open prairie, half a mile east of the village, repose the remains of Elijah Philips. And although no monumental inscription tells the spot where he so suddenly started for eternity, or " storied urn" adorns his grave; although of humble birth, yet he was a young man of much vigor and enterprise, and bid fair to become a useful member of society. Let his memory live " in story and in song," and be handed down to posterity with that of the other victims of savage cruelty.

No apprehensions are now entertained by the settlers, of attacks by the Indians. Black Hawk and his followers have gone beyond the Mississippi, and only a few remnants of Indian tribes remain in the whole State. Years will not efface the memory of the many deeds of extreme cruelty, committed by the Indians in this short, yet bloody war.   Acts of cruelty and outrage were perpetrated, too horrid and indecent to mention ; and so perfectly useless as it respected the result of the war, that they could have been committed only to glut a most fiend-like and savage vengeance.

I cannot admire the Indian character.   They are sullen, gloomy and obstinate, unless powerfully excited, and then, they exhibit all the antics of madmen.

After spending a few days viewing the country in this vicinity, I again crossed the river at Hennipen, and passed on to the stage road.   The next day, I took the stage, and went to Peoria, the county seat of Peoria county, which stands on the site of fort Clark.   This is quite a village.   It is regularly laid out on a beautiful prairie, on the western bank of the Illinois river ; has a brick court house, two taverns, a dozen stores, and about twenty dwelling houses, some of them quite elegant.   It is eighty miles from Ottawa, one hundred and sixty from Chicago, one hundred and fifty from Galena, one hundred and fifty by land and two hundred by water from St. Louis.

The river here swells out to more than a mile in width, and the opposite shore is low, marshy land. Peoria seems to be subject to bilious fevers and the fever and ague ; but I could perceive no cause for its being unhealthy, unless it was the river and marshy land on the other side.   The water is brought to the village in an aqueduct, from a high bluff, half a mile back of it, and appeared to be excellent. A number of deaths had occurred, previous to my arrival; and I saw a number of palefaced invalids.

In coming to this place, I passed over a fine country, much more settled, with larger fields and more extensive improvements than I found in the upper part of the State ; but still it was diversified with rolling prairies and groves of timber. While the mail was changing at one of the Post Offices, I passed on and came to a log school house, where all the scholars studied aloud. This was a quite a novelty to me. More discordant sounds never grated on the ear ; and if the master had a musical one, he must have been severely punished. I asked him, if his scholars commonly studied in this manner ; and he said they did, although he thought they now hollowed a little louder than usual. This inconvenient practice of some of our ancient schools, I supposed had been entirely done away ; but on enquiry, I was informed it still held its sway to some extent in many of the western States.

Stages run from Peoria, through Springfield, to St. Louis, to Galena, and to Chicago. There is a rope ferry just below the village, where the river is narrow. It is a place of a good deal of business, quite a thoroughfare for travellers; and it is supposed by some that it will shortly become the seat of the

6

State government. I spent three days here, then took passage on board a steamboat for St. Louis.

I have often remarked that the amount taxed by taverners is generally in an inverse proportion to their accommodations; that is, the less they furnish their guests, the more they charge. In my present trip, I have more than once been reminded of an anecdote related to me some time ago, of a tavern keeper at the south. A gentleman with his family, travelling in the westerly part of Virginia, was obliged one night to put up at one of the small country taverns, more suited to the accommodation of the teamster who sleeps in his wagon, than to the entertainment of gentlemen and ladies. They were furnished with the best the house afforded, but it was mean in kind and badly prepared. Some of them were obliged to sleep on the floor, and those that were accommodated with beds, were exceedingly annoyed by the insects they contained. The gentleman arose early, ordered his carriage and asked the landlord the amount of his bill. He told him, *thirty dollars!* The gentleman stared; but at length asked him, what he had had to the amount of thirty dollars, or even five dollars. The landlord very politely assured him that his was a reasonable charge, for says he, I hire this establishment at the annual rent of thirty dollars, and this I must charge to my customers; the year is almost out, and you are the only available guest I have had; therefore I have charged the whole amount to you. The gen-

tleman laughed heartily; and considering it too good
a joke to be spoiled by any fault on his part, very
pleasantly handed him over the thirty dollars. He
that travels much in the world, may have occasion
to fear the *rent day* is near at hand. This frank
explanation of the Virginia landlord has furnished
an easy solution to *some* tavern bills I have paid,
that otherwise would have been entirely inexplicable;
and perhaps it may be equally useful to other travellers.

The Illinois river is a wide, sluggish stream; clear
water, but generally, hardly any perceivable current.
It is a very shoal river, having many sand bars.—
Our boat did not draw more than two feet of water,
yet was continually running aground. I should
think the lead was thrown a quarter part of the
time; and it used to amuse me, sometimes, to hear
the leadsman sing out *"two feet and a half"*—
"two feet large"—*"two feet"*—*"two feet scant"*
—and then aground; and perhaps it would be half
a day before we could get afloat again. We were
seven days going to St. Louis—rather slow travelling, and somewhat vexatious; we thought, however, we might as well be merry as sad, so we made
the best of it. The captain had as much reason as
any of us to complain; for we took a cabin passage,
and he had to board us, however long the passage
might be. All along down, the country is rather
low, except some bluffs on the river—and where we
found a bluff on one side, there would be either a

low marsh or a lake on the other. Probably, there
are twenty lakes below Peoria, on one side or the
other of the river. They were all long and narrow,
and often had an outlet into the river. They appeared more like former beds of the stream, than
anything else.

Pekin is twenty miles below Peoria, on a high
bluff, the east side of the river, having two taverns,
thirty houses, and a large steam flour mill. Sixty
miles below this, on the same side of the river, is a
large village called Beardstown. Here are large
flour mills, saw mill, &c. all carried by steam.—
Twenty miles below this, is a small village called
Naples.

As we approached the Mississippi, we saw a good
many stately bluffs on the right hand bank, composed of limestone, and rising almost perpendicular,
from two to three hundred feet high. Some of
them are really grand and beautiful.

At length, with no small degree of pleasure, we
came in full view of the majestic Mississippi river.
The moment our boat entered the stream, it felt its
power, and started off with new life and vigor. It
seemed something like travelling, after leaving the
sand bars and sluggish current of the Illinois, to be
hurried down the Mississippi at the rate of eight or
ten miles an hour.

We soon reached Upper Alton, a large flourishing
village of recent origin. Here, are large steam flour
mills, and large warehouses; and in the centre of

business is located the State Prison! There is no accounting for taste; but it appeared to me rather singular, to see a prison of convicts brought forward into the centre of a village to be exhibited as its most prominent feature. The reason may have been, to keep it constantly in *view* as a "terror to evil doers." This is the last town we stopped at in Illinois—and on taking leave of the State, I may be allowed to add a few words respecting it.

More than half of the whole State is prairie. All the streams, lakes and marshes are lined with a fine growth of timber, sometimes a mile or two in width, and sometimes merely a narrow strip. And as the southern part of the State contains the most low, wet land, it has also the most timber. The high land is generally prairie; but there are some exceptions to this. I found quite a number of beautiful groves of timber on high land; sometimes there were only scattering trees, called oak openings.

The whole State is excellent land, having a black, rich soil, from two to four feet in depth; and beyond all question, there is less waste land here, than in any other State in the Union. I believe the upper part of the State more healthy than the lower part; but I also believe the State is quite as healthy as the State of New-York. Last fall was a sickly season throughout the United States; but Illinois suffered comparatively less than many of the other States. On the streams, it is found by experience to be more sickly than a few miles from them.

6*

The prairies are all burnt over once a year, either in spring or fall, but generally in the fall; and the fire is, undoubtedly, the true cause of the origin and continuance of them. In passing through the State I saw many of them on fire; and in the night, it was the grandest exhibition I ever saw. A mountain of flame, 30 feet high, and of unknown length, moving onward, roaring like "many waters"—in a gentle, stately movement, and unbroken front—then impelled by a gust of wind, suddenly breaks itself to peices, here and there shooting ahead, whirling itself high in air—all becomes noise, and strife, and uproar, and disorder. Well might Black Hawk look with indifference on the puny exhibition of fireworks in New-York, when he had so often seen fireworks displayed, on such a gigantic scale, on his own native prairies.

A prairie storm of fire is indeed terrific. Animals and men flee before it, in vain. When impelled by a strong breeze, the wave of fire passes on, with the swiftness of the wind; and the utmost speed of the horse lingers behind. It then assumes a most appalling aspect; roars like a distant cataract, and destroys everything in its course. Man takes to a tree, if he fortunately can find one; or, as a last resort, dashes through the flame to windward, and escapes with life; although often severely scorched; but the deer and the wolf continue to flee before it, and after a hot pursuit, are run down, overwhelmed and destroyed.

Much caution should be used, in travelling over
an open prairie country, in the fall of the year, when
the grass is dry. Instances were told me, of the
entire destruction of the emigrant and his family by
fire, while on the road to their destined habitation.

There are no *large* towns in Illinois, but quite a
number of flourishing villages. Danville, near the
eastern line of the State, is quite a flourishing town ;
and here the land office for the northern section is
kept. It is one hundred and fifty miles south of
Chicago, and it is supposed, that the office will
shortly be removed to that place. Springfield, situated on a branch of the Sangamon river, is near the
centre of the Sate, and is a large, flourishing village.
It is sixty miles south of Peoria, about thirty east of
the Illinois river; and it is highly probable that it
will become, shortly, the seat of the State government. The most important towns on the Mississippi river, are Galena, Quincy, Alton, Edwardsville,
and Kaskaskia; on the Ohio river, are Trinity,
America and Shawneetown; on the Wabash, are
Palmyra, Lawrenceville, Palestine, Sterling, &c. and
in the interior, besides those we have before mentioned, are Vandalia, the present seat of the State
government, Jacksonville, Maysville, Hillsborough,
Salem, and many other small villages ; besides quite
a number of *paper towns*, that may in time have a
" local habitation," in addition to their high sound-
ing names.

The State is favorably situated, in regard to navigable streams. It is nearly surrounded by water. It has the Mississippi on the west, the Ohio on the south; and the Wabash and Lake Michigan on the east; and nearly through the centre runs the Illinois river. All these furnish great facilities for transporting to market the rich products of its luxuriant soil.

I had heard much of the *backwoodsmen,* and supposed, of course, I should find many of them in Illinois; but after diligent search, I found none that merited the appellation. The race has become extinct. Who are the inhabitants of Illinois? A great portion of them, from the north, recently settled there, and of course, possessing the same hospitality, sobriety and education as the northern people. They went out from us; but they are still of us. A person will find as good society there, as here; only not so much of it. The upper house on Fox river settlement, was occupied by an intelligent and refined family, recently from Massachusetts.

Meeting houses and school houses are rare, owing to the sparseness of the inhabitants; but the country is settling rapidly, and these deficiencies will soon be supplied. Indeed, so rapidly is the country settling, that in writing this account of it, I sometimes feel like the man who hurried home with his wife's bonnet, lest it should be out of date, before I could get it finished.

Emigrants, going to settle at the West, with their families, would do well to take their beds, bedding, a moderate supply of culinary utensils, the most essential of their farming tools, and a good supply of clothing. These articles are all high there, and somewhat difficult to be obtained. The more cumbersome of household furniture, such as chairs, tables, bedsteads, &c. are not so essential; because their place can be supplied by the ruder articles of domestic manufacture. In the new settlements, most of the families had chairs or benches, tables and bedsteads, made on the spot by the husbandmen.

Provisions are cheap, but vary in price according to the demand. Corn, at Beardstown, is worth twelve and a half cents a bushel; at Hennipen, twenty-five cents; and on Fox river fifty cents; and other articles in proportion.

When the settler arrives at his location, his first business is to build a log house, which is soon done; then fence in a field, and it is ready for the plough. The prairie breaks up hard at first, requiring four yoke of oxen; but after the first breaking a single horse can plough it. A good crop is produced the first year; but better in succeeding years. He had better hoe his Indian corn. It keeps the ground clear of weeds, and increases the crop; but half of the cornfields are not hoed at all.

In the fall of the year, he must take especial care that his crops, stacks of hay, fences, &c. are not

burnt, in the general conflagration of the prairies.
To prevent this, as good a method as any is to plough
two or three furrows around his improvements, and
at a distance of about two rods plough as many
more; and in a mild day, when the grass is dry,
burn over the space between. If he neglects this,
he must keep a good look out in a dry and windy
day. If he sees a smoke to windward, it will not
do to wait until he can see the fire ; but must sum-
mon all hands, and set a back fire. With a strong
breeze, fire will sometimes run over the dry prairies
faster than a horse. The inhabitants are often too
negligent in this particular. While I was there a
number of stacks of hay and grain, and two or
three houses were burnt, from the mere negligence
of their owners.

But I must bid adieu to the beautiful State of
Illinois. To the practical husbandman, and to the
enthusiastic admirer of the beauties of nature, it is
alike attractive; and in which, they both will find
ample scope for the exercise of the powers of body
and of mind.

After two or three hours stay at Alton, we started down the stream ; and in seven miles came to
the mouth of the turbid Missouri. Here, two
mighty rivers join thoir forces, and rolling on with
irresistible power, for thirteen hundred miles, min-
gle with the waters of the ocean. The great Missouri, after traversing a vast extent of country, in
various directions, here bears directly down upon

the Mississippi; but the latter, like a coy maiden, shrinks back, recoils at his approach, and seems to decline the rude embrace; and they travel on together for forty miles, before the Missouri can unite its muddy waters with those of the clear and transparent Mississippi. Here, the Missouri, having at length gained the complete mastery, holds throughout its undisputed sway; and gives its own peculiar complexion to the united stream.

The appearance is, indeed, quite singular; to see the two rivers passing along, side by side, in the same channel, such a long distance, without mingling their waters; and the line, between the muddy and clear water, is so well defined and distinctly marked, that it can readily be seen from the shore.

On the western bank of the river, seventeen miles below the mouth of the Missouri, is the town of St. Louis. The view was fine and imposing, as we approached it by water; and it is the most pleasantly situated of any town on the banks of the Mississippi. It stands on an elevated plain, which gradually rises from the water, to its western extremity. Back of it, there is a level and extensive prairie. St. Louis is the most important town in all the western country; and there is not a town in the world, such a distance from the sea, that in commercial advantages can at all compare with it.— When we consider its situation, near the junction of two mighty rivers, the one navigable twenty-five hundred miles, the other one thousand, and the large

navigable branches of each, and see that this place
must be the centre of trade for the whole, it requires not the gift of prophecy to designate this
spot, as the site of the greatest city of the West.—
It is now a large town, chiefly built of brick; has a
brisk trade; and probably contains seven or eight
thousand inhabitants. There was a time, when the
only craft on the river was keel boats, and the transportation of goods, arduous and expensive. Then
this place struggled slowly into existence, and sometimes remained stationary, or rather declined; but
the introduction of steamboats started it into new-
ness of life and vigor. Its trade is now daily extending itself, and the town is continually increasing
in population and buildings. A dozen steamboats
were lying at the landing—some bound high up on
the rivers; others, to Pittsburgh and New Orleans.
This seems to be a sort of "half way house," between the upper and lower country; being a place
of general deposit for goods, destined either way.
And St. Louis will never have to contend with a
rival; for there is no other suitable spot near the
junction of the two rivers, to locate a city. She
will, therefore, continue to increase in size, wealth
and beauty, and remain in all time to come, the undisputed "Queen of the West."

The land in Missouri, for fifty or sixty miles bordering on the river, is rich in the extreme; but in
some places rather too low; and some of it, wet
and marshy. Beyond this to the west, it becomes

hilly and broken, and has a light, sandy soil. It is either very rich, or very poor. There is a land office kept at St. Louis; and plenty of government land to be obtained for a dollar and a quarter an acre. It is settled chiefly by Americans; but French settlers are found, and in St. Louis there are a large number. Considerable trade in peltries is carried on with the Indians, who come to the principal towns and exchange their skins for goods. They are continually seen in the streets of St. Louis.

St. Louis has a theatre, and we attended it.— Quite a decent edifice, a tolerable play, and a full and fashionable audience. I could perceive no essential difference between this assembly and those of Boston or New-York. Good society is found here. The streets at night were quiet; or only disturbed by the sound of the violin on board the flat boats, or the merry boatman's song. The sky was serene, the air mild, and we had many a pleasant walk through the town and its environs. Indeed, there is a peculiar balmy softness in the air, grateful to the feelings, not to be found in our northern climate. St. Louis is a pleasant place; and were it not for the stacks of bar lead on the shore, and some slight peculiarities in the customs of its inhabitants, it could hardly be distinguished from an eastern city. A steam ferry boat plies between this place and the opposite shore, and affords a large profit to its owner.

When we were ready to start, not finding a steam-boat bound to New Orleans, which would go under

7

a day or two, we took passage, as far as the mouth of the Ohio, in one bound to Pittsburgh.

On the eastern side of the river, to the mouth of the Ohio, it is a level country, (with only one exception) called the " American Bottom," and is as fine, rich land as earth affords ; but is somewhat subject to overflow, and is supposed not to be very healthy. Settlements are, however, making upon it.   On the west side we found a number of stately bluffs of limestone, rising from the water perpendicular two or three hundred feet.

I was much amused to see the " screw auger grist mills" on the bank of the river.   A place is select-ed where the current sets strong along the shore ; and a log seventy feet long, three or four feet in di-ameter, having a board float a foot in width from stem to stern, in a spiral form, like a coarse thread-ed screw, is thrown into the river.   To the upper end of the log, by an universal joint, is attached a cable, and the other end, extended in a diagonal di-rection to a shaft in the mill on the bank.   The log wheel floats in the water parallel with the shore, about a third of it above the surface ; is held in its position by sticks at each end extending to the bank, and the cable itself prevents its going down stream.   The current of the river turns the wheel, and the mill clatters merrily on the bank.

These high banks are not altogether without their use.   They furnish elegant sites for shot towers ; and probably half a dozen of them are thus occu-pied.

The greatest natural curiosity on the river, is what is called the " Towers." High pillars of limestone are seen on both sides of the stream, and one solid rock rises almost in the middle of the river, thirty feet high. Some of the most striking curiosities have particular, if not appropriate names given them ; such as " the grand tower," " the devil's candlestick," " the devil's bake-oven, &c.

The navigation of the Mississippi in steamboats has its dangers. Snags and sawyers are scattered along down the river ; and it requires great attention in the pilot, to avoid them. But there are other dangers beside this. As we came along down, we passed a steamboat that had burst her boiler ; blown the upper part of it to pieces and killed a number of persons ; and further down the Mississippi, the " Boonslick" run into the " Missouri Belle," sunk her in eighty feet water, and drowned a number of passengers.

As we came down opposite the mouth of the Ohio, we had our courage put to the test. It was about twilight, and cloudy ; but objects could well be discerned for some distance. We saw a steam-boat coming up the river, and apparently intending to pass us on the left hand. When within a short distance of us, the boat " took a sheer," stood on the other tack, to pass us on the right. Our captain sung out, " the boat is coming right into us ; back the engine." There was a scene of confusion and dismay on board ; " and the boldest held his breath for a time." If the boats came in contact, one or both would undoubtedly sink ; and it appeared unavoidable. I ran up on the upper deck, and stood beside the flag staff, to wait the event. It was soon decided. By backing our boat and putting the steam on to the other, we passed without striking at the distance of a few feet only. This was, indeed, a fortunate escape.

I thought the pilot of the other boat must have been to blame ; but the captain told me he was not at all. A cross current from the Ohio struck the bow of his boat, and veered her round in spite of the helm ; and then, the only chance was to go ahead with all the speed he could. It now became quite dark, and in attempting to go across into the Ohio channel, the boat run aground on a sand bar. All the boat hands were employed till past midnight to get her off, but without success. They all turned in, to rest and wait till daylight.

When the captain arose in the morning, he found the boat adrift. On examination, it appeared the force of the current alone had washed away the sand bar, and drove the boat across from the Mississippi side into the Ohio channel. He put the steam on, and we run to the landing place on the Illinois side, and a short distance up the river. Here we found half a dozen steamboats, exchanging with each other goods and passengers.

The mouth of the Ohio is a general stopping place for all boats running up or down either river ;

and would be a fine situation for a town, if the land were suitable to build upon. Although the shore appeared to be thirty feet above the then low stage of water, yet in a freshet, the whole is laid eight or ten feet under water.

We found here a large tavern house and grocery ; both stuck up on stilts ; the latter, standing nearest the bank, had a breakwater, to keep it from being carried away by the flood and floating timber. We stopped an hour or more ; went to the tavern, and found dissipation in a flourishing condition. Those acquainted with the place, told us it was as much as a man's life was worth, to stay there. Rioting, robbing, gambling and fighting were the general order of things, day aftrer day, and night after night. For the honor of the human race, I hope this account is exaggerated. But I must confess, appearances are against it.

Here, we left our boat, and took passage on board another, bound to New Orleans. These Mississippi steamboats are of gigantic size, and look like a floating castle—I was about to say the ancient ark ; and although it might fall some short of that ancient vessel, in quantity and quality of lading, yet when its size and great variety of cargo are taken into consideration, the comparison might not be deemed a bad one. In one particular, it would be exact. We had aboard a number of "*creeping things.*"

Our boat was laden with barrels of pork, kegs of lard, hogsheads of hams, bags of corn, bars of lead

7*

bales of cotton, coops of chickens, horses, men, women, children, and negro slaves; men of gentlemanly deportment and of good character; and gamblers, horse-jockeys and negro-dealers; and women, of good fame, ill fame, and no particular fame at all. This was, surely, variety enough for one boat.

The untravelled man might obtain some new ideas of the world, by taking a trip in a Mississippi steamboat. It seemed like a world in miniature.— Singing, fiddling, dancing, card playing, gambling, and story telling, were among the pastimes of the passage. Mere pastimes, to relieve the tedium of the voyage, for those who have no other resources at command, may not be the subject of censure; but there were some practices on board this boat, which ought not to be thus lightly passed over.

One woman, in the garb and mien of a lady, and whose person still wore the bloom of youth, but whose conduct was far from being unexceptionable, appeared, sometimes, pensive and sad. She appeared as though she had seen other and better days; and that her present course of life was not, even to herself, entirely satisfactory. I had some curiosity to learn something of her history, and one day in a talkative mood, she gave me the outlines of it.

She said, she was the daughter of rich parents in the State of Delaware. Her father died while she was quite young; leaving her with an ample fortune, and in the care of an indulgent mother. She had always been kept at school; learned music, drawing and dancing; read novels ; attended parties, and was caressed and flattered. In short, she was a giddy girl, and knew nothing of the world.

At this critical time of life, she was flattered by a young man of prepossessing appearance, but of worthless character, who offered her marriage. She knew her mother would, at her tender years, object to the match; and therefore, at the early age of fifteen, she clandestinely jumped out of the window of her boarding house in the night, and was married !

This was a sore affliction to her mother ; and although she herself was not entirely discarded, her husband was never permitted to enter the parental mansion. Her husband obtained her fortune, spent it " in riotous living," and after awhile, left her with two small children, and fled to Cincinnati. She, in her distress, applied to her mother ; she would receive her, but not her children. She then took her children and went after her husband. She found him ; but they lived but a short time together, before he abused her in such a manner, she was obliged to quit him ; and not much caring whither she went, she took passage on board a boat for St. Louis. At this place, she supported herself and children as long as she could, by selling her trinkets and superfluous clothing, and then was left destitute. She had never been accustomed to labor ; her hands were as delicate as those of a child—she " could not work and to beg she was ashamed." As a last resort, (could a virtuous woman think so?) she became an inmate of a house not of the *strictest morals*.

After staying there awhile, she became acquainted with some of the hands of the boat, who persuaded her to try her fortune at the city of New Orleans. She was now only about twenty! She was miserable, and expected to be so. Vice carried with it its own punishment. I tried to induce her to return to her mother; but in vain. Her conduct had been such, she was ashamed to return. A sad termination this, to the bright hopes, and fond anticipations of an indulgent mother. So true it is, that one improvident step in life, often leads to destruction.

Another female who figured somewhat conspicuously, was one who came on board at the mouth of the Ohio from the steamboat Nile; and from that circumstance, was called by the passengers the "queen of the Nile." She was from the State of Ohio, possessed a fine person, and in her days of innocence, must have been handsome and fascinating. She was the daughter of respectable parents, and commenced life with high hopes and brilliant expectations; but she had been "disappointed in love." Abandoned by her "cruel spoiler," she gave herself up to dissipation and crime. The bloom of her cheeks began to fade, and the sad aspect, sometimes so conspicuously depicted in her countenance, plainly indicated a mind ill at ease and a heart pain-

fully sad. She travelled without object, other than
to revel in dissipation and kill time. But her course
of life had made serious inroads upon her health,
and it was apparent enough that her days must be
" evil and few." I sometimes observed her sitting
on the guard of the boat for hours all alone, gazing
in sadness at the peaceful forest and cottages as they
passed in rapid review before her, the tears fast
flowing from her eyes, and her face exhibiting such
anguish as may not be expressed by words. She
kept on in the boat to New Orleans, and I afterwards was informed by a gentleman who was a fellow passenger, that she became mistress to a French-
man in that city. How mistaken mankind are !—
Crime never did cure the heart ache, or dissipation
ever dispel sorrow.

The steamboats are constructed like a long two
story house, having large windows and green blinds.
The hold is to stow away their heavy freight ; on
the first deck, is the gentleman's cabin, and the dining room, where all the cabin passengers take their
meals ; in the centre, is the engine, cook room, &c.
—and forward, are the boilers and wood. On the
next deck, is the ladies' cabin aft, and forward is the
place for deck passengers, having berths but no bedding. Over this, is what is called the " hurricane
deck."

A cabin passage from St. Louis to New Orleans,
is twenty-five dollars ; and a deck passage seven
dollars—the passenger finding his own bedding and

meals.   Cooking stoves are provided, so that families often lay in their own provisions and cook their
own meals.

Boats burn a good deal of wood—ours consumed
a cord an hour; and it is no small job to bring the
wood aboard from the slippery banks of the Mississippi.   As an inducement to the deck passengers to
help wood the boat, two dollars are deducted to
those who agree to wood; so in that case they only
pay five dollars.   Thirty or forty of our passengers
agreed to wood, but the mate and clerk had much
difficulty to make them fulfil their engagements.

It was sometimes really laughable, to see the ex-
pedients resorted to, to get rid of wooding; especially when the boat rounded to, by the side of a
wood-pile in the night.   The clerk would sing out,
" wood-pile, wood-pile, where are the wooders ?"—
But they, like some characters in high places, were
more inclined to " dodge the question," than to walk
up manfully and perform their duty.   Some feigned
themselves sick ; some hid under the baggage, or
beneath the berths; others went on shore and skulk-
ed in the woods, until the wooding was over.   So
that with all their coaxing and driving, they would
not be able to bring to the work more than half of
the wood hands.

One fracas was ludicrous, although I could not
but regret the result.   It is well known, that the inhabitants of the several western States are called by
certain *nicknames*.   Those of Michigan are called

wolverines; of Indiana, *hooshers;* of Illinois, *suckers;* of Ohio, *buckeyes;* of Kentucky, *corn-crackers;* of Missouri, *pukes,* &c. To call a person by his right nickname, is always taken in good part, and gives no offence ; but nothing is more offensive than to mis-nickname—that is, were you to call a hoosher a wolverine, his blood would be up in a moment, and he would immediately show fight. Now it so happened that the mate, who was a regular built buckeye, had a dispute with a wood hand, who was about half drunk, and refused to wood. The mate stood on the lower deck, and he on the deck above; and in the course of the wrangle, he had called him some terrible hard names, which he bore with becoming fortitude and forbearance. At length, the wood hand called him a " d—d old puke !" This was too much—unendurable. He fired in a moment—rushed up and floored him in a twinkling— dragged him down by his collar, thrust him ashore, and left him in the woods.

But the steamboat, the steamboat! For noise and confusion, give me the Mississippi steamboat. They all have powerful high-pressure engines; the escape pipe is large, and at every breath they make a tremendous noise. They " talk big," and swiftly dash through the water. It is indeed a grand display, to see the steamboats pass. In " a voice of thunder" they come—the wheels lash the water— and the prows cut the stream—and the waves roll in violent commotion for hundreds of yards behind them. And then, the noise of the engine, and hurry and bustle of the passengers within :—an excellent place to cure one of the ennui.

On board our boat, we had a number of very intelligent and agreeable gentlemen—Kentuckians, Tennesseans, Mississippians, &c. I wish these western people would be a little more exact in speaking the English language. Some inaccuracies I observed ; and if this book ever reaches them, they will not be offended, but obliged to me for these suggestions. In the first place, they use the word *which* instead of *what*. Ask a question, and if they do not understand you, they reply " *which ?*"— Another phrase, " I have *saw*," instead of "I have *seen*," is often used. Then there is " a right smart chance," applied to almost every thing ; and " tote in the plunder," instead of " bring in the baggage." But the word *heap* has too much by far *heaped* upon its shoulders. " A *heap* better," " a *heap* easier," and " a *heap* of ladies," are phrases often heard. I may be a little sensitive, but the word *heap* is very disagreeable, and I wish it was expunged from the English vocabulary. All these expressions are not used by many literary men in this country, but they are indeed, quite too common.

They have some peculiarities in the calling of money. A New-England *ninepence* is called *a bit ;* and the four-pence-half-penny bears the name of *pickaroon*. In travelling from New-Hampshire to Virginia some years ago, I was somewhat amused at the different names given to the same piece of money. My four-pence-half-penny became at New-York a *sixpence*, at Philadelphia a *fip*, and at Virginia it became a four-pence-half-penny again. But all these singularities and inconveniences will soon be done away, and money will universally bear its legal title, dollars and cents.

There is an independent frankness in these western people that I admire. It is a kind of individuality of character—every one appears to act out himself, without reference to others. At the north, people are too apt to follow the multitude, or a particular file leader; and by them, shape their opinions and actions. In order to tell whether they will do a particular act, they must look about them, and ascertain what others will say of it. The politician must conform to the usages of his party, whatever they may be. He must think as they think, and act as they act, whether it be agreeable to the dictates of his own consience or not. The pious lady must be exactly in the fashion—conform to certain leaders—be charitable by rule—and kind, in the most approved mode. If any one has the boldness to take an independent course, in fashion, politics or religion, he is looked upon with suspicion, as a dangerous innovator, and must not be tolerated. The dogs of war are let loose upon him, and he is hunted down for entertaining an opinion of his own. In this manner, individual character becomes swallowed up and lost in that of the multitude.

8

But in this region, nature is true to herself. The useless and cumbersome shackles of custom and party are thrown aside with disdain; and the individual walks forth in his own native freedom and independence. He does not shape his course by what his neighbors may say, do or think; but acts according to the dictates of his own heart, and from his own opinion of right and wrong. He is charitable, kind and hospitable—not in a grudging, supercilious manner; or in a way calculated to display himself; but with such an air of open-hearted welcome, as to make the recipient feel at ease, and doubles the value of the kindness bestowed. How can man be niggardly and mean, among the teeming prairies and stately forests of the West, where nature herself, by showering down her blessings with a bountiful hand, teaches him also to be liberal!

And I have often to myself reversed the question and asked, how can northern people be other than inhospitable and niggardly, living in such a crabbed climate, and on such a barren soil. They cannot, in general, afford to be liberal; and were it otherwise, the severe labor and economy—the continual dealing in small things—the constant rack of brains, to find some method to turn a penny to advantage—that must be gone through with, to gain a large estate, seem to drive out of the head of the possessor all notions of liberality, and tend to steel the heart against noble acts of kindness. That which costs much, and is rarely obtained, is highly valued, and not lightly parted with. We are not well educated in the school of hospitality. We awkwardly perform its teachings—seldom with gracefulness and a hearty welcome.

Among our passengers, there were twenty-three negro slaves, men and women; bought in Kentucky by negro speculators, to be transported to Natchez, where the market is high, to be sold. One of them was taken with the cholera, and in twelve hours died. He was put into a rough box, and when we stopped to wood, buried on shore. This was the only case we had, and the only one I ever witnessed. It is a dreadful disease; but has been too often professionally described, for me to attempt it.

These negroes are singular beings. Although one of their number had died; and although they were slaves, and going to be sold to, they knew not whom, or what hardships they might be made to endure, yet they were always merry—talking, laughing, singing, dancing, in one continued round. At every place we stopped, they would run on shore, and while one sung, clapped his hands, and beat time with his foot, the others would foot it merrily on the smooth ground. Knowing their destination, their thoughtless gayety sometimes produced disagreeable sensations. There are some situations, however, where ignorance and thoughtlessness are a blessing. They were not confined at all, but appeared to be kindly treated, and to enjoy every liberty they might, consistent with their situation.

The banks of the Mississippi look high enough at
low water; probably thirty feet; presenting a raw
edge next the stream, and generally covered with a
dense forest of lofty trees; yet at high water, they
are generally overflowed, except at the high bluffs.
The most prominent of these, are what are called
the Iron Banks, Chickasaw Bluffs, Walnut Hills,
and the site of the city of Natchez—all these are
on the east side of the river. I do not remember
of seeing a single high bluff on the west side, below
the mouth of the Ohio.   There are occasionally
small elevations over which the river does not flow ;
and villages erected on them.   But every few miles
without regard to overflows, log houses are erected
in the wilderness, inhabited by wood-cutters; and
their only employment seems to be, to supply the
steamboats with wood.   Although wood is cheap,
being generally $1,50 a cord, above the mouth of
the Ohio, and from there to Natchez $2,00, yet
the demand is so great, and the forest so near, they
make quite a lucrative business of it.

The river is very crooked, sometimes going five
miles to gain one ; has many islands, and some
places, full of snags.   There are two or three snag
boats employed on the river, and when they get them
chiefly out, the Missouri, which seems to take upon
itself the chief regulation of the stream, brings
down at high water a reinforcement equal to the
first supply ; so that to keep the river clear of snags,
is like the labor of Sisyphus, who was doomed to roll

a stone up a hill, and the moment he got it near the top, it would roll down again.

The introduction of steamboats on the western waters, has revolutionized the country. They have opened the deep recesses of the West, to the free access of mankind, and let in the light of day upon them. The half-horse and half-alligator race are no longer to be found; but the inhabitants of this part of creation look, and talk, and act, and live—very much like human beings. The refinements, elegancies and luxuries of life are not so generally found here, as in the Atlantic States; but all the necessaries are every where abundant.

In Michigan, Illinois, Missouri, and all along the river Mississippi, I found the inhabitants civil and kind; and in no one instance did I ask for a meal of victuals in vain. It might, sometimes, be a homely one, and once I recollect, it consisted of meat and bread; but those who have such a mawkish sensibility that they cannot relish the simple fare of the forrester, ought never to set a foot on the western world.

The flat boats are still in use on the river. We passed hundreds of them; some loaded with live stock, others with corn, cotton, &c. They have hardly any resemblance of a boat. They are sixty or seventy feet long, ten wide, having corner posts and a square form like a house, and a flat roof. The current floats them down the stream to the destined

8*

port, the cargoes and boats are both sold, and the hands take passage on board the steamboats, home.

We stopped at all the villages and towns of any size on the river, to take and leave passengers and freight ; but books give such an accurate description of them, as to render any particular notice here unnecessary. Memphis is the most pleasant, Vicksburg the most flourishing, and Natchez the largest —all on the east side of the river.

There are no large towns on the west side of the river below the mouth of the Ohio. As prominent as any, perhaps, is New-Madrid, situated just within the southern border of the State of Missouri. It was once a much larger village than at present. It is memorable for the romantic history of its origin under General Morgan, and for the great earthquakes in 1811 and 1812. Mr Flint says that these earthquakes were more severe than any known in our part of the continent. These shocks were felt more or less throughout the whole western country ; but they were more severe and produced the most disastrous effects in the region of New-Madrid.— The grave yard of the village, with all its sleeping tenants was precipitated into the river—the trees were violently thrown against each other, bent in various directions or prostrated—the earth burst in many places, and earth, sand and water were thrown high into the air—thousands of acres were sunk and many ponds formed—the river became dammed up and flowed backwards—islands sunk in the stream and boats as they passed shared the same fate—the birds of the air became terrified, descended to the earth and flew into the arms of man to shelter themselves from the commotions of nature—the whole country for a time became inundated, but as it was thinly inhabited few lives only were lost. History does not record an earthquake attended with more terrific circumstances and threatening a more exterminating war with man and nature, than this. The thriving country about the village was made desolate, but now it is slowly regaining its former condition. In this region the country is rich and beautiful, but the many ponds made by the earthquake render it unhealthy. New-Madrid is, however, quite a village, transacts much business and is the most noted landing place for steamboats on the west side of the river below St. Louis.

At Natchez, I left the boat, and stopped a day or two, to make the necessary preparations to go over land on horseback to Texas. There is a steamboat that plies regularly between this place and Alexandria on Red River; and we should rather have travelled by water as far as that place, and avoided crossing the Mississippi swamp by land; but the boat had gone, and would not return under a number of days.

Natchez is an incorporated city, containing about three thousand inhabitants. That part of it which lies under the bluff near the river, is muddy, looks old and disagreeable; but the main part of the city

is situated on a high bank, two hundred feet above
the river; chiefly built of brick, quite pleasant, and
makes quite a show of business. The ground back
of it, is full of gullies, and is unpleasant. It is an
old town, but has much improved within a few years.

Many people going to Texas continue on down
the river to New Orleans, and there take a passage
on board a vessel to some port in the province; but
my desire was to see the country, and therefore, I
chose to travel over land. A pleasant and companionable gentleman from the State of New-York, who
came down in the boat with me, agreed to bear me
company. Some acquaintances of his, with their
families, were on the road to Texas, and he like myself wished to see the country.

Having provided ourselves with horses, portman-
teaus, fireworks, &c. and obtained the necessary directions, we took an early start; crossed the Mississippi in a ferry boat, for which we were taxed half a
dollar each; and took the road to Alexandria. We
had some ill-forbodings about the great Mississippi
swamp; for just as we were about to cross the river,
a gentleman, of whom we made some enquiries respecting the route, told us he thought it now impossible to travel through it in consequence of the rains
which had recently fallen. But we were all equipped to go by land, and this, our only route; and
therefore, we determined, at all events, to push forward.

There is a road from the mouth of Red river, along its bank to Alexandria, and this, we were afterwards informed, is the best route ; but it was seventy miles below us ; and whoever takes it, must go down in a boat.

Our route lay, for the first six miles, up the river near its bank ; and then we turned more to the west. We passed half a dozen cotton plantations, some quite large, and saw an army of negroes picking it.

The cotton plant grows about as high as a man's head, has blossoms about as big as that of a small rose, and resembling in appearance the hollyhock, but more extensive branches. The pods are about the size and shape of the outer covering of a walnut ; and when ripe, it opens in quarters, and presents the cotton in full view. A negro takes a basket or a bag, and swings it at his side, and with his thumb and finger picks out the cotton, almost as fast as a hen picks up corn. It grows from the seed, is planted every year in hills like corn, and cultivated in the same manner.

A field of cotton in full blossom, makes a fine appearance. After it is picked, it is laid on a rack to dry ; then ginned to take out the seed, and put up in bales for the market. The rope and bagging used, are the manufacture of Kentucky ; or at least it brings more into market than all the other States. I was told that one prime hand on good land would *make* ten bales of cotton a year, and raise corn enough to support himself. The average worth of

these bales is five hundred dollars. From enquiries
I afterwards made, I believe the plantations generally make about seven bales to the hand. No wonder negroes are valuable in a cotton-growing country.

Our route now lay through a dense forest—and
the ground generally so miry that we could only
ride on a walk. Sometimes we came to the thick
cane-brakes, about twenty feet high, and overhanging our narrow path. Sometimes, we found the
palmetto, which exactly resembles a large green,
open fan, standing on a stem a foot high, and so
thick that we could hardly ride through them, or see
any path at all. Sometimes, we came to a sheet of
water one hundred yards wide, in which a horse
would plunge to the saddle skirts, and for awhile,
become stuck fast; and again, we would find a cypress swamp, full of cypress knees and mud. Indeed
it is the worst swamp I ever travelled over, before or
since ; and sometimes, I thought our horses were
stuck too fast ever to move again.

These cypress knees are quite a curiosity. They
start from the roots of the tree, grow from two to
four feet high, about the size of a man's arm, but
rather larger at the bottom, and are smooth, without
leaf or branch. They look like a parcel of small
posts with the bark growing over the top end ; and
are so thick, that it is troublesome to ride among
them. The cause or use of this anomaly in nature
I cannot divine.

Eighteen miles from Natchez, we came to two log houses and a small stream, called the Tensaw We crossed the ferry, about twice the length of the boat in width, and paid half a dollar each for ferriage. We had now twelve miles to go to find a stopping place for the night, and all the way, through a dense forest of lofty trees; and it was three o'clock in the afternoon. The first half of the distance was decent travelling, although we could not ride much of the way, faster than a walk. Then we came to a wet and miry road.

It began to grow dark in the woods. The trees were quite thick, and hung full of Spanish moss; and there was no moon in the sky. The wolf, the wildcat, and the owl, had pitched their tune for the night; and soon, thick darkness shrouded around our path. The heavens were clear; yet so dense were the foliage and moss, that it was seldom I could find a loop hole, through which a star might cast its rays upon us. I never had been in such a gloomy situation before. We were in a path, to us untravelled; and by its appearance, seldom travelled by man. We had shoals of muddy water to cross, and sloughs of mud to wallow through. And then the night was so dark, and the track so faint, we frequently lost it, and found it again with difficulty. It was ten o'clock at night when we arrived on the shore of a lake, and saw a light on the other side.— We raised the ferryman after awhile, and he came out and took us over.

This lake is about a mile wide, and twelve long, and must have once been the channel of the Mississippi. The ferriage here was half a dollar each. On the other side, we found a good house, and a genteel family within. They soon provided for us an excellent supper, which was very acceptable after a ride of thirty miles over such an execrable road. Not being much used to travelling on horseback, I felt excessively fatigued and retired immediately to bed. My companion and myself had each of us a good bed, and we slept soundly until after sunrise.

The morning was fine, so we walked awhile along the shore of the lake, before breakfast. It was about the twentieth of November, yet the air felt as mild as a morning in June. The winter was following hard after me, yet I had travelled to the southward and westward faster than the cold weather. The coldest weather I had found on my route, was in the state of New-York. There is a softness in the atmosphere of the western States that is very grateful to the feelings, and is not found in our northern climate. In going westward on the same parallel of latitude, the air becomes sensibly more mild and bland. The air is very clear, so here as in Illinois, I could discern objects much further than at the North. I could see a house so far off, that it would not look larger than a bee-hive. There had been no frost here, and nature wore her livery of green.

This gentleman has a fine cotton plantation of rich alluvial land. His house is built facing the lake, on an Indian mound, levelled down to the height of about six feet. We took breakfast with the family in a large portico on the back side of the house. It was a good breakfast, on a neat spread table, and the lady at the head performed the honors of it, with an ease and grace seldom equalled. We performed our parts to a charm, both in eating the breakfast and complimenting the hostess.

This family were from the State of Virginia, and had been settled here in Louisiana seven years.— The gentleman informed me they had generally enjoyed good health, although they had sometimes been afflicted with the fever and ague.

It is refreshing to the weary traveller, when far away from his home, to find a bright spot in his path, where he can renew his strength, and repose in peace. At such a spot he lingers, leaves it with regret, and treasures it up in his memory.

I have often thought, that many persons do not travel in a right spirit. They start on their journey with a full belief that all the customs and modes of life they find, differing from those they have been accustomed to, are all wrong, and proper subjects of censure and dislike. They see nothing in its true light, enjoy nothing, find fault with everything ; and are continually running their heads against a post. They are always on the rack ; and probably punish themselves as much as they do every one around

9

them. But such a course betrays gross ignorance. Who can read the outpourings of madame Trollope's brain, without being convinced that she had too gross conceptions, and too strong prejudices, to write the history of any people, whose manners were different from her own. She saw nothing, only through a jaundiced eye; and she had too narrow and contracted a mind, ever to make the important discovery, that the fault might be in herself, and not in the objects with which she was surrounded.

Some prefer to be mere scavengers; and when they find anything gross or impure, delight to exhibit it to the gaze of the world. I have often thought of the severe reply of Dr. Johnson to a lady, who told him she liked his dictionary, because he had no indelicate words in it. O, says the doctor, I did not trouble *my* head about them, but I see *you* have been looking for them.

Other travellers think, the more fault they find, the more they will be noticed ; and they will be treated with the more deference and respect. I once happened to ride in the stage with the venerable Chief Justice Marshall. He was affable and polite, at peace with himself, and displeased at nothing. In the same stage, as if nature intended to exhibit two beings in bold relief, and make the contrast the more striking, was a testy young man, who found fault with every thing, and was pleased with nothing. He cursèd the driver, the stage and the road ; and the country through which we travelled was too

execrable to live in. At the hotel, where we stopped to dine, he kept the house in a continual uproar.
The dinner bell rang, and we sat down at the table.
For some reason, he did not come in immediately;
and when he made his appearance, the table was
entirely full. This was too much for him to bear.
He cursed the waiter for not saving a place for him.
The waiter, as quick as possible, provided him a
place at a side table. But he was determined not
to be thrown into the shade in this manner. The
Judge ate his dinner in silence; but this *side table*
gentleman kept a continual cry for something. " I
say, waiter"—bring me this, and bring me that.—
His vociferations became quite annoying. At length,
he cried out with rather increased vehemence, " I
say, waiter, bring me a *fresh* potatoe." The moment this was uttered, one of the gentlemen at our
table said, " Waiter, give that gentleman a *fresh*
chair, I am sure he has set in that one long enough."
This was a damper. It caused quite a laugh at the
young man's expense. He became silent, and after
dinner, we saw no more of him.

" Behold us mounted once again,"—and immediately after leaving this gentleman's plantation, we
again passed into a dense forest and found a muddy
path. In about six miles we found some sandy
land and pine timber, and here we left what is called the Mississippi swamp. We soon came to the
outlet of the lake, which we had to ford. The
water was deep, and the shores deep mud. It was

a difficult job to make a horse wallow through. We were told that a horse got swamped and died in the mud, a few feet from the spot where we crossed.

We came to the banks of Washita river, followed it down three miles, and crossed over to Harrisonburg. The town is built on a level plain on the west bank of the river; but it contains not more than twenty houses. This river empties into Red River, and is navigable for steamboats a long distance above the village. It is forty-two miles west of Natchez. On this river are the lands where the famous Aaron Burr *talked* of establishing a colony; but unless the land above and below is better than in this region, it might not have been very flourishing. The soil is too sandy and poor.

We rode twenty-five miles over a rolling sandy country, generally covered with pine woods; and stopped at night with a gentleman who had been one of Burr's party. He did not seem inclined to say much of that ill-fated expedition. Here, we were kindly treated, and fared well. He had been there nineteen years; had cleared a large plantation; raised cotton, corn and cattle; had eight or ten negroes, and possessed the necessaries of life in abundance. But he still lived in a log house, without a glass window in it. I asked him, why he did not have windows. He said, the house was well enough; if the hole cut for a window did not make it light enough, he opened the door. It was not just such a house as I should be contented in, for

nineteen years, and possessing the wealth he had.—
It, however, was to his taste ; and for aught I could
see, he was as happy as those who live in much better houses.

To-day we travelled thirty-three miles to Alexandria, just one hundred miles from Natchez. The
first forty was Mississippi swamp, excellent land, but
a good deal of it too low for cultivation ; the last
sixty miles was, with few exceptions, hilly, sandy,
pitch pine woods. We passed only a few good plantations. Occasionally, we found a small prairie of
poor soil, and a deserted log house. It was indeed
the most dreary road I ever travelled. In the last
day's travel, we passed two small rivers ; one we
crossed in a ferry boat ; and to our special wonder,
we found quite a decent bridge over the other.

Red River is rightly named ; it is almost as red as
blood, caused by the red soil through which it passes.
It is quite a large stream ; but the water is too brackish to drink, or for culinary purposes. The only
resource of the inhabitants of Alexandria is to catch
rain water, for which they have enormous large cis-
terns. We crossed the river opposite the town in a
ferry boat, and found the current about as strong
as that of the Mississippi. It is navigable for
steamboats, in a moderate stage of water, as high up
as " the raft," and when the removal of that is completed, for a long distance into the country. About
a mile above town, there is a short rapid which boats
cannot pass when the water is low.

9*

The mouth of Red River has probably undergone some changes. It is almost certain, that in by-gone years, Red River had its own separate channel to the Gulf of Mexico; but in process of time, the ever changing Mississippi river took a long turn that way; struck into its channel, and after appropriating its waters and three miles of its bed to its own use, wheeled round to the left, and pursued its own course to the ocean. In this state of the case, the upper part of Red River became a tributary of the Mississippi, and the lower part a mere waste-way to pass off its superfluous waters. But the inconstant Mississippi, a short time ago, cut out for itself a new, straight channel across the bend, and left Red River to itself. This cut-off, however, proved of incalculable advantage to that section of country. It let off the Mississippi waters so freely, that a large tract of most excellent land does not now overflow; and this is sought for with avidity, and settling fast.

Alexandria is pleasantly situated on a level plain, the south side of Red River, one hundred and four miles from its mouth, and three hundred and twenty-nine from New Orleans. It is regularly laid out in squares; has a court house, three hotels, eight or ten stores, two or three groceries, and a number of good dwelling houses. Its chief export is cotton, and that of the first quality. Red River cotton commands the highest price in market. I saw a large number of bales piled on the river bank, and wagon loads coming in.

Gentlemen and ladies, in pleasure carriages and on horseback, were riding through the streets; and the hotels were full of guests. It appears to be a place of business and of pleasure; of much wealth, and in a rich neighborhood. This place and Natchitoches, seventy-five miles above it, are the only towns of any size in this section of the country.

At the upper end of the town, there is a regular laid out race-course, of a circular form, and a mile in extent. Here, the speed of horses is frequently put to the test, and extensive bets made on the result. This seems to be the favorite sport of this country—of more absorbing interest than any other; and about which the people talk more than on any other one subject. Good race-horses are of great value, and almost any price will be given for them. Although the race-course may have its great attractions—it may exhilarate the feelings, to see that noble animal, the horse, with mettle high, and lofty bearing, spurn the dust beneath his feet, and skim along the plain with the swiftness of the wind; and although it may have a tendency to improve the breed of horses; yet upon the whole, may it not be said, that it is purchasing improvement and pleasure, at a great expense of time and money; and, independent of its moral effect upon society, productive of more evil than good.

Gambling is too much the order of the day. A large billiard room faces the main street in this village, and seems never to lack for customers. In

this room one man killed another by striking him on
the head with the *cue*, and his trial was just finished
as I arrived.   He was convicted of manslaughter,
and sentenced to ten years confinement in the State
Prison.   The result of the trial gave general dissat-
isfaction among the people.   They thought he ought
to have been convicted of murder and suffered its
penalty.

Not much attention is paid to the cultivation of
vegetables or fruit.   The peach and fig-tree were
the only fruit trees I saw, and but few of them.—
The fig-tree much resembles our northern quince
tree, but grows some larger in size.   The only
vegetables we had at table, were turnips and sweet
potatoes.   The northern potatoe will not produce a
crop unless new seed is obtained every year.

All the beds in this region are surrounded with
thin curtains, or as they are termed here, moscheto-
bars, to protect the inmate from that pestiferous,
anti-sleeping insect, the moscheto.   Of all insects
this world produces, the moscheto is the most troublesome and annoying.   To lie down without a bar,
as I sometimes did, and fight the moschetoes all
night long is dreadful.   Too tired and sleepy to
keep awake, I would fall into a drowse, only to be
aroused in a moment by half a dozen dabbing into
my face, and singing in my ears.   They are indeed,
too familiar by half; and the only chance to cut their
acquaintance is to flee.   I would not spend my days

in the region of moschetoes for the sake of wealth;
for I should only possess splendid misery.

About a mile above this place, we left Red River,
and travelled the road on the bank of Bayou Rapide
for twenty-five miles, to the mansion house of a Mr.
Henderson, where we stayed over night. In this
day's ride, we passed over as rich land as I ever saw,
covered with extensive cotton plantations. It is all
river-bottom land of a red clayey soil; and all along
the road, as we passed, we saw clouds of negroes
with bags and baskets at their sides, picking cotton.
The land produces an abundant and a profitable
crop, and the planters appear to have grown rich.—
But it seems not exactly to be a paradise, if there
be indeed, any such a place on earth. It is excessively annoyed by moschetoes, and is very unhealthy.
During the warm, sickly summer months, the planters with their families flee to the pine woods, where
the air is fine and salubrious; and leave their overseers and negroes to battle with disease and moschetoes, the best way they can. They are very
companionable, hospitable and kind, and their style
of living is much the same as that of the southern
planters generally.

About half way up, we crossed the stream over
a bridge to the right hand side; and just before we
arrived at Mr. Henderson's, we crossed it again.—
Soon after we crossed it the first time, I happened
to cast my eyes towards the stream, and found it
running the other way! We had certainly been

travelling all along up the stream ; and now, without any apparent cause, either in "the lay of the
land," or direction of the channel, it was just as
certain its current was with us. I enquired of our
host the meaning of all this. He pleasantly observed, that the streams in this part of the country, were
very accommodating ; they could go almost any
way. He, however, explained the phenomenon.—
He said, the channel of the stream, by the side of
which we had travelled, was, undoubtedly, once the
bed of Red River. Ten miles above him, the river
had taken a straight course to Alexandria, and left
its former circuitous route. The water, which we
now saw running, is supplied by a stream from the
lake, enters the old channel on the opposite side
from where we were travelling, then divides itself,
one half running down and entering the river near
Alexandria, and the other running up the old bed,
and entering the river ten miles above. When the
river is high, a portion of it flows round in its old
bed, and drives the upper current along with it. So
that by his house the stream runs about half of the
year one way, and the other half in the opposite direction ! A rather difficult stream I should think,
to build a mill upon. This is indeed quite a curiosity ; but to the explanation one objection may be
urged. If this be in fact the old bed of Red River,
and from examination I am satisfied it is, one might
naturally suppose it would be all along descending
one way ; and, therefore, the stream which enters it

would not divide itself, but the *whole* of it run in the *same direction* that the river formerly did. The answer to this is, the stream coming in, carried sand with it, and for a considerable distance somewhat filled up the old channel, so as to make a descent each way ; but not so much as to prevent Red River when high, from sweeping round, in its former course.

A curiosity, in some respects similar to this, is found in Arkansas territory. White river and Arkansas river enter the Mississippi ten miles apart ; and about twenty miles above, there is a direct water communication between them ; which is a large navigable stream ; the water of which runs, sometimes one way and sometimes the other, according to the comparative height of each river ; so that a person living on its bank, could make no sort of calculation which way the stream might run, from day to day.

Mr. Henderson has a large house pleasantly situated on a sandy hill near the pine woods, and commands an extensive view in front of the river flatland, and cotton plantations. We here fared well ; and as Mr. Henderson has ample accommodations, his house may be safely recommended as a stopping place for the traveller. Our route now lay through the pine woods. Our object was to strike the road from Natchitoches to Mexico, at the nearest point practicable ; and this spot, we were told, was at the garrison, fort Jessup. This fort is situated half way between Natchitoches and the Sabine river, the line. between the United States and Texas ; being twenty-five miles from each. Natchitoches being twenty-five miles north of our route, we concluded not to pass through it; but when Red River is high, travellers to Texas often take a passage on board a steamboat from Natchez to that place, and from thence, take the Mexican road.

From Mr. Henderson's, an intelligent gentleman, well acquainted with the country, travelled with us three or four days on our route; and from whom we obtained much information. This day, we travelled forty miles through an unbroken forest of pitch pine. The land is sandy, gently undulating, but seldom rocky. The trees were of good size, but not so thick together as to prevent the grass from growing beneath them; or the traveller from seeing a great distance as he passes along. About half way, we found a small log house, in which a white man lived with a black wife. With some people, I suppose this would be thought commendable ; but I confess it gave me unpleasant feelings to see half a dozen of *half-bloods* running about the house. He professed to keep a sort of tavern, but all the refreshment we obtained was bread and meat.

At night, we came to the house of a planter, near a small river. He had a hundred acres cleared of river bottom land, which had been planted with cotton and corn ; a large stock of cattle and hogs, which ranged in the woods. He had lived here twelve years, was worth twenty thousand dollars; yet still, lived in a log house with only two rooms, and without a window in it. Our supper was fried beef, fried greens, sweet potatoes, corn bread and a cup of coffee, without milk or sugar; which we ate by the light of the fire, as he had neither a candle or a lamp. Our fellow traveller told us, that we had now got out of the region of what we should call comfortable fare; and we might expect to find it worse, rather than better, all the way through Texas. Our lodging was on a comfortable bed made of Spanish moss; and our breakfast exactly like our supper, which we ate with the doors open to give us light. Our bill was a dollar each, for supper, breakfast, lodging and horsekeeping; and this, I found to be the general price, in all country places throughout Texas.

After passing the river and about a mile of bottom land, we came to the pine woods again. I could always tell when we approached a stream, by the trees being covered with Spanish moss. The first I saw, was on the Mississippi, about a hundred miles above Natchez; and in all the region south of that, it is found hanging to the limbs of the trees near streams of water. It is of a silver-grey color, hanging straight down from the limbs three or four feet, like a horse's mane. It looks, perhaps, more like dressed flax than any thing else; and some of the trees were so completely covered with it, that we could hardly discover any thing but the moss. It

10

does not strongly attach itself to the limb. I used to pull off handfulls of it, as we passed along, to examine. It is but the work of a few minutes to gather enough for a bed. The only preparation necessary is to scald it in hot water, or to let it remain awhile in cold water, to rot like hemp. It then looks like fine long hair, and of a dark brown color. When dry, it is whipped, and put into the tick. It makes a very good, cheap bed, and lasts a long time. Of this material most of the beds in this country are made, and sometimes a mattress of the kind is found at the north.

All the river bottom lands at the south, are covered with a dense, heavy growth of trees, among which are many kinds not found at the north. The cotton-wood grows very large, somewhat resembling the white-wood of the western States. The magnolia, celebrated for its large, splendid blossom, is an evergreen, having a dark green leaf an inch and a half wide, and two and a half long, and of the size of the maple—the peccan, a tree resembling the walnut, and bearing a round nut an inch long, equal to the hickory-nut—the hackberry, about the size and much resembling the beach—the holly, a small evergreen, having a small thick leaf—the chinquopin, a mere shrub, resembling the chesnut tree, and bearing a similar but smaller nut. We frequently found the grape vine of large size running high up the trees ; and occasionally, a spot of cane-brake.

This day's travel was through the pine woods, except at some few places where we found a small clearing and a log house, near some small stream.— We did not go by fort Jessup. Our companion knew of a nearer route, and we took it. About the middle of the afternoon, we came out on the Mexican road, three miles south of the garrison. It appeared to be a road a good deal travelled by wagons, as well as on horseback; some places running through swamps and muddy; occasionally, a bridge over the most miry streams; but generally in a state of Nature. The land became some better, and we passed more settlements.

At night, we stopped at a log house kept by a widow. She had, living with her, two sons and one daughter. The house had no windows, and but one room in it. Near it, was a small kitchen where a negro woman did the cooking. Our fare was very similar to that of the night before, except the old lady had a candle on the table at supper. There were four beds in the room, where we all slept—the old lady and her daughter in one bed—her two sons in another—and we three travellers in the other two. I hope the delicate nerves of my fair readers may not greatly be disturbed at this; if they are, they must close the book, and read no further; for if I must tell " the whole truth," I shall be obliged to state, that during the thirty following nights, I often slept in the same room with one or more ladies !

The old lady had about twenty acres cleared and cultivated with corn ; but the land is not the first rate. The fact is, all along Missouri, Arkansas and Louisiana, after you get sixty or seventy miles west of the Mississippi river, you come to light, sandy, hilly land ; generally covered with pitch pine ; excepting a narrow strip on the margin of the streams ; so that half of Missouri, three-fourths of Arkansas, and half of Louisiana, are poor land, hardly fit for cultivation. This is not what I had supposed ; but from my own observations, and the information of travellers, I believe this to be the fact.

We took an early start, and travelled on. The northern people have been accused of being very inquisitive ; but I am sure I would turn out the people here against them on a wager. As a general rule, we were inquired of " where from"—" where going," &c. &c. To-day, a man, twenty rods distant from the road, came running up, and asked us, where we were from. I thought this was carrying inquisitiveness too far ; and so I took the yankee privilege of answering his question by asking another, viz ;—If it was out of mere curiosity, or for the sake of obtaining information beneficial to himself, that induced him to enquire. He said, he was from Kentucky himself, and did not know but we might be from there also ; and in that case, he wished to enquire the news. I told him we were none of us from Kentucky. But this did not satisfy him ; he insisted upon knowing where we were from ; and appeared quite vexed that he could not obtain the information from any of us.

We passed a number of covered wagons, generally with four horses, loaded with goods and families bound to Texas. They invariably lodge out doors over night. They carry their own provisions with them, and select some spot where there is plenty of wood and water, build up a fire, cook their meals, turn their horses or oxen loose to feed on the prairie, or in the woods, and camp down on the grass by the side of the fire. I saw some who had been thirty and forty and sixty days on the road ; from Missouri, Illinois, Indiana, &c. and said they had not put up at a house for a single night. Some of them looked quite " wearied and worn ;" and if they do indeed find rest at last, it must be confessed, that " through great tribulation" they enter the promised land.

About noon to-day, we came to the Sabine river, the dividing line between the United States and Texas. We had now travelled from Natchez two hundred and twenty-five miles on horseback ; and this, the seventh day since we started. I had now become used to the saddle ; and saving the muddy roads and miry streams which we sometimes found, I enjoyed the trip very well. I was surprised to find the Sabine so small a river. I should think it was not more than one third as large as Red River. It is a deep muddy stream, and gentle current. We

10*

were paddled across the river by a woman, who was a " right smart" one, and landed at last on the shore of

TEXAS.

I had read and heard so many fine descriptions of Texas—its pleasant streams, beautiful prairies, mild climate, and extensive herds of buffalo, wild horses and cattle, that it was with no small degree of enthusiasm, I set foot, for the first time, on its territory. I cast my eyes back for a moment on the United States ; then turned to the " fairy land," with high hopes and bright anticipations.

The Sabine has two or three miles of good bottom land on each side, heavily timbered ; but it is too much subject to inundation to be cultivated.—— After we passed the river bottom, we came to gentle swells, of red clayey soil, covered with oak, hickory, &c. called oak openings. Sometimes we passed a small prairie ; and, occasionally, a log house and a small field. Thus we passed ten miles ; and here, our fellow traveller, having arrived to the end of his journey, left us. He had travelled a hundred miles with us ; was an intelligent man, well acquainted with the country, and we became too much interested in him, not to feel serious regret at parting. This is one of the disagreeable things in travelling ; we form acquaintances only to leave them.

We now found cotton fields, as well as corn ; more extensive plantations, and better houses. We passed two race-courses by the road side, and stop-ped for the night, at a very decent looking double log house, having a wide portico in front, and a wide avenue through the centre. Here, we found good accommodations. The house contained three or four rooms, and had about the same number of glass windows in it. We had for supper, venison, sweet potatoes, corn bread, coffee, butter and milk. Back of the house, I observed a small orchard of apple trees, the only one I found in all Texas. The trees looked thrifty, and had just begun to bear fruit. In front, near the road, was as fine a spring of good, clear, soft water, as I ever saw; but it was hardly cold enough for a northern man. Here were exten-sive fields of cotton and corn. This planter had a cotton gin and press. The cotton was sent by land to Natchitoches; to be transported from thence to New Orleans by water.

Six miles from this, we came to an entirely new village, called St. Augustine, near a stream called the Ayish Bayou. About two years ago, it was laid out; and now it contains two large taverns, three stores, a court house, and ten or a dozen dwelling houses. There is a good school kept here, to which scholars are sent from some distance. It would be tedious, however, to relate the particulars of this, and the two succeeding days—it would only be the same story over again. Our fare was rather poor—the meals, better than the lodging.

One night, we slept in a new framed house, one side all open to the weather; and the other, we slept in a log house, the interstices between the logs not filled up, so that you might thrust your arm out almost any where. This night we had a smart shower, accompanied by a strong wind, and the rain beat in so liberally, I was obliged to haul my bed eight or ten feet to leeward. We passed quite a number of log houses, small plantations, through oak openings and pine plains, and, at length, came to the ancient town of Nacogdoches.

I could not but smile at the odd and grotesque appearance of Nacogdoches, as I entered the principal street of the town. In by-gone days, the Spaniards built a town of log houses; generally having the logs standing perpendicular at the sides and ends, and the space between them filled with mud; with chimneys made of the same materials. These look old and woe-begone. In modern times, the Americans have erected a number of elegant, framed houses, well finished and painted white; and these are scattered along among these ancient hovels. The contrast is very striking, and somewhat ludicrous. Before me, stood an ancient Roman Catholic church, built in true Spanish style, with perpendicular logs and mud; now falling to decay, and presenting to the eye a hideous mass of ruins.

The town stands on a beautiful plain; having a small stream of water on each side; is very healthy; and when American industry shall have removed these dark spots from its surface, will be a most desirable place in which to reside. It has two public houses; and the one we put up at, had very respectable accommodations. There are a number of stores, which carry on a brisk trade with the country people and Indians. The chief article the Indians have to sell is deer pelts; and in the course of the year, they bring in a large number. These are done up in bales, and sent by land to the United States.— These skins are bought of the Indians by weight, and, I was told, the average amount was about fifty cents apiece. I observed a number of Indians in town on horseback; and this is the general mode of travelling, for all the western and southern Indians.

Nacogdoches is the head quarters of the " GALVESTON BAY AND TEXAS LAND COMPANY." The lands of this Company embrace three grants; that of Zavala, Burnet and Vehlein, and are bounded on the northeast by the Sabine river; on the northwest by a small river called the St. Jacinta; on the south by the Gulf of Mexico—about one hundred and seventy miles in width, and running northwest nearly three hundred; equal to fifty-one thousand square miles. I shall now continue my journal, and give hereafter a description of this Company's lands in my general view of Texas.

While at this place, I frequently saw Maj. NIXON, the agent of the Company for giving titles to the grants. He is quite an agreeable and intelligent man, and very readily gave me all the information respecting the country that I requested. No more than a league of land is granted to foreigners ; but to the Spaniards, a number of leagues are frequently given. The Spaniards, however, place but little value upon land. They sometimes have large flocks of cattle and horses ; but are too indolent to cultivate the soil. Quite a number of them reside at Nacogdoches ; some very respectable families ; but a good many are poor and indolent. They are of a darker complexion than the Americans, and are readily designated at first sight.

An instance of the little value placed upon land was stated to me while here. An American had a fine looking dog that a Spaniard took a fancy to ; he asked the price, and was told, a *hundred dollars.* The Spaniard replied, he had no money, but would give him a scrip for *four leagues of land !* The bargain was immediately closed ; and the land could now be sold for $10,000. Truely the old adage, " *dog cheap*," ought to be reversed.

Immediately after leaving the town, we came into pine woods again ; to all appearance, the same we had already passed over—rolling, sandy soil ; the trees straight and tall, but standing so far apart, that a carriage might go almost any where among them. The grass grew beneath them, and we could see a great distance as we passed along. And thus it continued, for about twenty miles, with hardly a house on the way. I thought, we never should have done with pine woods. We had travelled about three

hundred miles from Natchez; and two-thirds of the
way, had been pine woods; and here, they made
their appearance again. To ride a short distance
in them, is not unpleasant; but to continue on, day
after day, is too monotonous—there is no change of
scenery.

In twenty miles, we came to an elegant house,
painted white, a large portico in front; a neat paling
round the yard, and large fields beside the road. A
saw and grist mill were building on a small stream,
about a mile from the house. We passed a small
river over a bridge, having split rails for a covering,
instead of plank, and through pine woods, oak
woods, and small prairies, and put up at a house
near the bank of the river Neches, forty miles from
Nacogdoches.

By the side of the road near his house, I saw a
race-course, and the gentleman told me there were
frequent races on it. He had himself won twelve
hundred dollars on a bet, a short time before. His
house was made of hewn logs and clapboarded,
having three rooms in it, but as usual in this country,
no windows. We had our common fare, beef, corn
bread and coffee.

On a large prairie in front of his house, I saw
two Indian mounds, and as I had a little leisure before breakfast, I went out to examine them. I had
seen many of the Indian mounds in the western
States and Louisiana; and these were similar to
them. The largest one was about twenty feet high

and ten in diameter. I was puzzled to find where the dirt was taken from to make them, as the ground was a perfect level a long distance around; but my host showed me the spot about half a mile distant, and from the size of the excavation, I thought he was right. No reason can be given, however, why the dirt was carried such a distance.

I have seen no satisfactory explanation given of the origin and use of these mounds. Some say, they are places of interment; others say they are sentry stations, on which guards were placed to watch the movements of the enemy. Who built them? The present race of Indians know nothing about them—make no use of them—and build none like them. Now, if their ancestors built these mounds all over the country, it is utterly impossible to believe that all tradition would now be lost of such prominent monuments, which passed in review before their nation, from day to day and year to year. I am decidedly of opinion, that their ancestors did not erect these mounds; but that they were built by a more civilized race of men, inhabiting the country anterior to them. So far as I am informed, they are found nowhere except near some navigable stream; and, at this late stage of the world, their origin and use may never be fully and satisfactorily explained.

We found the Neches to be quite a river; clayey banks and muddy water. We saw a boat on the other side; and a house half a mile distant, through the woods. We could not tell whether it was ford-able or not; but after calling a few times for the ferryman, my companion concluded to plunge in. I thought in that case, discretion was the better part of valor; so I waited to see what became of him, before starting myself. He had a good horse, and although the stream was deep, and quite a current, he came safely out on the other bank; sustaining no other damage than being decently wet. He was good enough, however, to loose the boat, come over and take me across; remarking that there was no great pleasure in fording streams like that. We now passed through ten miles of pine woods; then prairies of a mile or so in extent, and post-oak open-ings.

This was the thirtieth day of November. The day was warm and mild, although somewhat cloudy. As we were passing through the woods, it became quite dark. On casting my eyes on the sun, I found it was under an eclipse. It was here, almost total. I thought it hardly lacked a digit of being entirely covered.

We stopped at night at a small log house on the side of an extensive prairie. We found only a young woman at home. She said, she was from the east part of Texas, had been married only a week, and moved there a few days previous. Her husband soon returned. He had been to spend the day, it appeared, at a neighbor's, seven miles dis-tant, and left the new made bride at home alone.—

11

All we obtained here to eat, was meat and corn
bread, and water to drink ; and that not very good.
He had sixty or seventy head of cattle, twenty cows ;
but no milk, butter, or cheese. He had quite a
large field under cultivation, in which he raised corn
only. He had a hired man to help him take care of
the flocks and the field, and to accompany him in
his hunting excursions. A number of skins were
stretched out on the sides of his buildings, as the
trophies of his prowess and success ; among which,
I noticed the skin of a large panther. In the morning, his wife went a quarter of a mile for water,
picked up wood and built a fire ; and the two men
looked on and did nothing. What young lady
would not marry, if she could pass such a honey-
moon as this !

The next day, we passed three houses, a number
of prairies and post-oak openings ; but found no
more pine woods. Immediately on this side of the
Trinity, we passed over a low, wet prairie, four
miles in extent ; where a horse would sink in to the
fetlock joint ; and then, half a mile of heavy timber. The Trinity is a large stream ; but not quite
as large as Red River—deep, navigable, and muddy
water. We stopped at the house of an intelligent
farmer on the other bank of the river. Here, our
accommodations were very good. He had a house
of hewn logs, three rooms, no windows, a portico
in front and rear, and an avenue through the middle.
The front yard was fenced in ; and a kitchen and

smoke house were in the back yard. He had a large field cultivated with corn, and perhaps, half a dozen negroes.

I here found a young man, who deserved commisseration. He was from Missouri. With his young wife and two small children, the youngest not quite a year old, he started in a wagon for Texas. He had been two months on the road; encamped out in the woods every night, although they had some wet and chilly weather. The fatigues of such a long journey, and the many attentions such small children required at the hands of the wife while on the route, were more than her constitution could endure. She became worn down almost to a skeleton; and grew daily more enfeebled; but as they were approaching the end of the journey, she kept up a good heart, and exerted herself to the utmost. But " tired nature" could do no more. She sickened and died—and left her husband in a distant land, with two infant children. Those who have endured the agony of a parting scene like this, although surrounded by relatives and friends, may form some estimate of the measure of pity due to him!

There are many hardships, perplexities and sufferings, necessarily attendant upon a removal to a new and distant country; and any accident or misfortune is more severely felt, because a person has no chance of remedying the evil. I do think, a single family ought not to go to a new country alone;

but a number in company ; and then they can assist
each other in all their hardships and trials.

At the mouth of Red River, a gentleman, moving
on to Texas with his family, lost his pocket-book,
containing about four hundred dollars.   He carried
it in the breast pocket of his coat; and in unlading
some of his goods from the steamboat, he stepped
forward to assist, pulled off his coat, threw it across
the railing, and the pocket-book dropped out into
the water and sunk.   It would have swam on the
water, had it not contained three or four dollars in
specie.   Search was made for it ; but the stream
was so deep and muddy, they were foiled in all their
attempts to find it.   This was, at such a time and
in his situation, a severe misfortune.   On the road,
two thousand miles from the place he started from,
and five hundred more to travel; his family with
him, and all his money gone.   A family of his acquaintance happened to be in company with him,
and through their assistance, he was enabled to proceed.

Another case was stated to me, more aggravating
than this, because it was not the effect of accident
but of knavery.   A gentleman, moving from Michigan to Texas, brought down in the boat a valuable
horse worth three hundred dollars.   On board, he
became acquainted with a young man, who wished
employment, and he hired him.   When they arrived
at the mouth of Red River, he concluded to send
his horse by the young man across the country by

land, and he and his family would go round by water. He, accordingly, equipped the horse with a new, elegant saddle, bridle, martingale and saddle bags; and supplied the young man with a good greatcoat, and twenty dollars in money, and started him off. And that was the last time he saw man, horse or equippage! He incidentally heard, that a man answering his description, gambled away a horse and equippage at Alexandria.

For ten miles after leaving Trinity river, we passed over some most beautiful rolling prairies. Although it was December, yet the air was mild and serene, and the grass as green as in June. These prairies much resembled those of Illinois; and on some of them, we saw large flocks of cattle feeding. We passed some miry swamps and deep muddy streams. The most disagreeable part of the whole trip, was the fording of streams. The banks were generally steep down into the water; and so slippery, we had sometimes to dismount, hold on to a tree, and let the horse slide down; then pull the horse beside us, mount him in the water, and ride across. I would sometimes take my saddle bags off, send my horse over by himself, and find a tree or a log on which to pass myself. The water was very muddy, so that we could not see the bottom, or form hardly any idea how deep it might be, until we forded. One stream was a very bad one. There were logs in the bottom, embedded in the mud about the middle of the river; and when our horses passed

11*

them, they struck into a channel where the water was about two feet deeper; their heads were suddenly plunged under water, and we came very near being thrown into the stream. Among the trees in the swamps, I noticed the red cedar, to-day, for the first time. It grows to quite a large tree, and is very good timber for building, boards, posts, &c.

To-day, we found by the side of the path a number of petrified limbs of trees; and in one place, there was a log about a foot in diameter, turned into stone. We broke off some pieces which plainly showed the grains of wood; and on one side the bark remained and was petrified also. It might probably be manufactured into good hones, although it was coarser grained, and of a lighter shade, than those usually found at our stores.

We passed only two houses this day, and put up for the night at a miserable log house occupied by a widow woman. She had a large stock of fine looking cattle, but no milk. Our fare was not of the best kind, although the old lady tried to accommodate us well as she could.

There are few mills of any kind in the whole country. The corn is ground in a steel mill, like a coffee mill, although much larger, and having a crank on each side. This is commonly nailed to a tree before the door. The corn is often left standing in the field, and gathered only as fast as they wish to use it. It used to amuse me, when we rode up to a house at night, and called for a meal, to

hear the woman sing out to a boy, " Run to the
field and bring two or three ears of corn—I want
to make some bread for the gentlemen's supper."—
So we had to wait until the corn was gathered,
ground, kneaded and baked, before we could have
bread to eat. I suppose this is the true method of
" living from hand to mouth."

We took an early start the next morning, and after
passing swamps, streams and woods, came out into
a fine prairie country. Our path led over the top
of one, somewhat elevated above the general level
of the country, and from which we could see many
miles all around. It was a prospect too grand and
imposing to be adequately described.

As we passed along by the side of an extensive
prairie, we saw two Indians horseback, on an elevated spot, about half a mile distant, with guns in
their hands, and looking at the country beyond
them. On seeing us, they wheeled their horses and
came at full speed down upon us. We were a little startled at first; but they halted within a few
rods of us, stared a moment, and then civilly passed
the time of day, and enquired in broken English,
the distance to a house on the road we had come.
I never was an enthusiastic admirer of the Indian
character. They may have done some noble deeds
of daring, and performed some generous acts of disinterested friendship; but they possess and practice
the art of deception so well, that no one can know,
with any degree of certainty, when these acts may

occur. When I see Indians approaching, I hardly know whether it is for good or for evil; and therefore, never feel entirely at ease in their society.

The Romans, in the days of their prosperity, prided themselves in being called a *Roman citizen*; and this was generally, a sufficient protection from depredation and insult, when travelling among the more barbarous nations around them. Like the Romans, I felt not a little pleasure in the thought, that I was an *American citizen*, and that this was a protection from outrage and insult in the presence of the savage Indian. Since my return, I have seen an account of twenty Polanders, while on their way from New Orleans to Mexico, who were attacked by the Indians in Texas, and all killed except one, who was fortunate enough to escape and tell the story.— Had not the Indians readily discovered by our personal appearance, that we were *American* citizens, we might have shared the same fate.

We passed a muddy swamp, in many places the water standing in the road a foot or two in depth; densely covered with timber, and four miles in extent. As we emerged from this, we came upon the bank of the Brazos river, at Hall's ferry. This is a stream of the size and complexion of Red River.— In crossing in a boat, we found a strong current. On the other side there is a high bank on which a town has been laid out; but now contains only three dwelling houses and one store. Here we stayed over night. Late in the afternoon, a Spanish tra-

der arrived and put up for the night. He had two
men, five mules and one horse and wagon with him.
His goods were bought at Natchitoches, and he was
transporting them to St. Antonio in the interior of
Texas. They were made up into convenient bundles, hung across the mules' backs and stowed in
the wagon. They were all armed with guns; and
the trader himself had a pistol at each side. He
could not well talk English and we conversed but little with him. He had a strong dislike to the Indians,
and was afraid of being robbed by them. Of this
ill-will, the Indians have their full share. In hunting parties composed of both Americans and Spaniards, when attacked by the Indians in their excursions along the Rocky Mountains, they have been
known to spare the Americans, when they have killed all the Spaniards.

The next day's ride was through a most beautiful,
open prairie country. We crossed some small
streams, skirted with timber and small groves on the
highland; but generally, we found high, rolling
prairie. The live-oak made its appearance to-day.
This is an evergreen and a beautiful tree. We saw
them growing on the open prairie, sometimes, one
standing by itself, about the size, and at a distance,
of the appearance of the northern appletree.

On a fine high prairie, we observed quite a number of elegant houses, a store, tavern, &c. and some
fine farms. This is called Cole's Settlement; and
from the beautiful scenery around, and the respecta-

ble appearance of the inhabitants, I inferred that it is a desirable neighborhood.

We stopped for the night at a house half way between the Brazos and Colorado rivers; being thirty-five miles from each. A few years ago, a town was lotted out in this place, but still it shows only one decent farm house. Here is a grist mill turned by horses, and does a good deal of business; and profitable too, for the rule is to take one sixth part for toll. In the neighborhood, I saw a very good looking house, built of limestone.

From this place to the Colorado river, we passed only two houses; a distance of thirty-five miles; and the complexion of the country was similar in all respects to that of the day before. At a very decent farm house on an extensive prairie, by the side of the river, we put up for the night; and remained here and in the neighborhood, a number of the succeeding days.

And now, from this central position, I propose to take a more general view of the country. I stayed more than a month in Texas, traversed the country in various directions, conversed with the inhabitants, and gained what information I could within that time. I feel, therefore, somewhat qualified to speak of the country. And this I shall do fearlessly; yet I hope, in sincerity and in truth. I am aware that many articles have been written concerning this country, of various import and meaning; but I shall speak for myself only, without reference to others.

I do not propose to write its geography or history. Had I the means and ability accurately to do this, the limits of this work would not allow of it. I only propose to give the information I obtained from inspection, examination and enquiry, in a concise form and tangible shape.

GENERAL VIEW OF TEXAS.

From whatever point you approach Texas, its aspect is unfavorable. If it be by sea, you are met by a low, sandy beach, and a marshy, flat country, as far as the eye can reach. If by land, through Louisiana and Red River, its first appearance is that of a poor country of hilly land, chiefly covered with wood, and presenting to the eye a weak soil, alternately of sand and of clay. But when you pass the border towards the interior, the scene becomes entirely changed. You behold a beautiful country of rich soil, rounded by the hand of nature into the most fanciful forms, covered with eternal verdure, and begirt with forests of stately trees. Earth may not afford a more beautiful prospect than is obtained from the summit of an elevated prairie. On such a spot I have stood, and gazed with admiration. The scene extends all around as far as the eye can reach, and presents the varied aspect of wood land and lawn, like sunshine and shade. Its appearance is so much that of a country nicely cultivated by the hand of man, that one can hardly believe himself to be in an uninhabited region; but he looks in vain, to catch a glimpse of the husbandman's cottage, and his herds of cattle feeding on the green fields.— The din of human industry and civilized life strikes not his ear, and the unwelcome truth is forced upon him at last, that he is only in the solitude of the wilderness; and the scene before him, with all its beauties, is left " to waste its sweetness on the desert air !"

The scenes of Texas have so much of fascination about them, that one is disinclined to come down to the details of a common-place description of the country. But the whole truth must be told. The public have a right, and in fairness ought to know, the true state of the case. The emigrant cannot live on air, or by admiring the beauties of the country. It is of importance to him to know, what facilities the country offers, for obtaining the necessaries and conveniencies of life ; and what the prospect may be of enjoying them, when obtained.

In the first place, I shall strike off from the list of the resources of the country, "the immense herds of buffalo and wild horses." They are often paraded in the many published descriptions of Texas, as a most prominent feature in the bright picture exhibited ; and as one of the many inducements to the emigrant to remove thither. But they are no sort of benefit to the settler at all. They generally keep ahead of population, some small herds only are ever seen near the settlements; and there is not inducement enough for the husbandman to leave his farm, and go far into the interior, to catch the wild horse and kill the buffalo, among tribes of hostile Indians; as the prospect of gain would not equal the hardship, risk and expense. The wild horse is an animal hard to catch; and when caught, it is difficult and troublesome to tame him, and render him gentle and kind in harness and under the saddle. It would be as well for the farmer if the fact of their existence were not known; as it is easier to raise the animal in this country of ever-green pasture, than to catch and tame the wild one. There is one point of view, in which a knowledge of the existence of these animals may be of some importance to the emigrant; it is proof positive of the natural luxuriance of the soil, and of the mildness of the climate.

The wild horses are called by the Spaniards, *mustangs*. I saw some small herds of them prancing at random over the plains. They are quite wild, you can seldom approach very near them. They are of various colors and of rather smaller size than the American horse. The Spaniards are fond of good horses, and are good horsemen. Some of them make a business of catching and breaking the mustangs. This is done by building a fence in the shape of a harrow, with a strong pen at the small end, and driving them into it; or mounting a fleet horse, get as near as they can unperceived, then start after them at full speed, throw a rope with a slip-noose at one end, and the other fastened to the sad-

12

dle, around the neck, haul out at right angles with their course, and choke them down. When caught, they put the bridle on, take them into a large, soft prairie, mount them at once, flog them with the greenhide, and let them plunge and rear until they become fatigued and subdued. After undergoing a few more operations of this kind, they are deemed "fit for use." They are sold at various prices, from six to twelve dollars; but unless they are caught when young, they never become gentle as other horses.

Texas appears like the State of Illinois. To the southward and westward of Trinity river, it is generally an open prairie country. All the streams have more or less bottom land, covered with a dense forest of timber; and occasionally, a grove of post oak openings will be found on the moist high land. The soil in these bottoms is very rich, but some ·of them are too wet, or too subject to be overflowed to admit of cultivation.

A strip of land, bordering on the bays and sea coast, and sixty or seventy miles in width, is flat, generally approaching to a dead level, in the spring and fall very wet, and sometimes, impassable. Beyond this, comes the high, dry, rolling country, having no swamps except immediately on the borders of the rivers. "The Galveston Bay and Texas Land Company" have a good deal of good land, in pleasant and healthy situations; and much of it, not yet settled; but they have also a good deal of poor land.

In their grant, are large tracts of pine woods and post-oak plains; among which, are found some spots of good land, but generally, it is of a weak and sandy soil. The pine woods are not without their use. Their resinous qualities give a salubrity to the air about them, and thereby render a situation in their neighborhood healthy ; and the trees themselves furnish an inexhaustible supply of the first rate of timber. On the Sabine and Galveston Bays, there are large prairies of good land, but low and flat; in the region of Nacogdoches, are small prairies, large tracts of wood, good soil of red clay, black marle, sandy land, and all the varieties of soil imaginable. Higher up in the country, there are alternately prairies and wood land, and an excellent soil. This Company's grant lies contiguous to the United States, and except on the bay, is as healthy as any part of the country; but it cannot be called the most pleasant and beautiful portion of Texas.

The prairies are all burnt over twice a year—in mid-summer, and about the first of winter. Immediately after the burning, the grass springs up again ; so that there is an abundant supply, all the year round. No country in the world can be compared to this, in the ease and facility of raising stock. All the herdsman has to do, is to look after them, so they may not stray away, and some portion of the year, yard them to prevent their growing wild. The prairie grass is of a peculiar species, unlike any thing we have at the north ; but it is of so

nutricious a quality, that it keeps the cattle fat, all
the year round. They grow large and handsome.
I never saw better looking herds in my life. The
horse does equally as well on grass, but if worked
hard, requires some grain. Hogs keep in good flesh
all the year; and in autumn, when the nuts fall
from the trees, grow fat. Horses, cattle and hogs
can, therefore, be kept in this country without any
more trouble than merely looking after them to prevent their straying away.

And then, there is plenty of game. First in the
list, is the deer. I hardly supposed there were as
many deer on the continent, as I saw in Texas.—
They were continually crossing my path, or were
seen in flocks feeding on the prairies. I recollect
that from an elevated spot, I counted five flocks of
deer in sight at the same time! In some parts of
the country, a man may about as certainly kill a
deer if he choose, as a northern farmer can kill a
sheep from his flock. Their meat is excellent, and
their skins valuable.

Deer-hunting is not very systematically practised
here, as it is in some parts of the world. Indeed,
they are so plenty, that it does not require much
method, or concert of action among a number of
individuals to kill them. The deer is a gregarious
animal. You never find one alone, unless it be accidentally strayed away from the flock. Sometimes
a number of hunters resort to a favorite haunt of
the deer, and while a part of them arouse them

Shooting deer.

with the dogs in their retreat, and cause them to
flee, others will remain in ambush near their usual
crossing places at the streams and swamps, and
shoot them as they pass. In the night, they are de-
coyed by fire and killed. A hunter fixes a blazing
torch in his hat, or has another person to carry one
just before him; the deer will stand gazing at the
light while he approaches, and by the brilliancy of
their eyes and space between them, calculates his
distance and takes his deadly aim. He must take
especial care, however, that the shadow of a tree or
of any thing else does not fall upon the deer; for
in that event, he starts and is off in a moment.

Then there are the bear, Mexican hog, wild geese,
rabbits and a great variety of ducks. The prairie
hen is not so plenty here as in Illinois. An emigrant may, therefore, easily supply himself with
meat. All he has to do is " to kill and eat."

Let us now glance at the soil, and see what that
will produce. This subject I attended to, somewhat
critically. It will produce cotton, sugar cane, Indian
corn, rye, barley, oats, rice, buckwheat, peas, beans,
sweet potatoes and all common garden vegetables.—
The cabbage does not form a compact head as it
does at the north. Wheat will *not* grow in this
country. The stalk will run up rank, but the ear
will not fill with plump kernels. Last December,
while I was there, flour sold on the river Brazos, for
ten dollars a barrel; and in the interior, it sold for
fourteen. Corn grows well, and is quite a sure crop
12*

when planted early—about the first of February.
I saw a very good crop which had been planted in
June.

I found one man, who, with the aid of a boy ten
years old, raised and gathered fifteen hundred bushels of corn.   Perhaps I am severely taxing the cre-
dulity of my readers; but if there be any reliance
on human testimony, the fact is as I have stated.—
And when it is considered, that the ground is only
ploughed, a small portion, if any, hoed at all, and
then it gets ripe early, and he can gather it at his
leisure—the statement may not appear at all incred-
ible.   Tobacco will grow, but it has too thin a leaf
to be valuable.

But it is emphatically a cotton country.   It produces a larger quantity to the acre, and of a better
quality than any portion of the United States—not
excepting the bottom lands on Red River.   This is
my belief from an examination of the growing crop
and gathered cotton.   And I found this to be an
admitted fact by the most experienced cotton grow-
ers.

The following is as perfect a list of the forest
trees, shrubs, vines, &c., as I can make—to wit:—
Red, black, white, willow, post and live oaks; pine,
cedar, cotton-wood, mulberry, hickory, ash, elm, cypress, box-wood, elder, dog-wood, walnut, pecan,
moscheto—a species of locust, holly, haws, hackberry, magnolia, chinquopin, wild peach, suple jack,
cane-brake, palmetto, various kinds of grape vines,

creeper, rushes, Spanish-moss, prairie grass, and a great variety of flowers. The live oak, magnolia, holly, pine and cedar are ever-greens.

The Spanish moss, so profusely hanging on all the trees near streams of water, gives them an antique and venerable appearance. It is of a silver grey color; and, if trees may be compared with men, they appear like the long grey bearded sages of the antedeluvian world. When the tree dies, the moss soon withers, and becomes dry. I used to amuse myself by setting fire to the dry moss in the night. It burnt like tinder, and would sometimes throw a grand column of flame a hundred and fifty feet into the air, and brilliantly illuminate the scene, a great distance around.

Of fruit trees, I saw only the peach, the fig and the orange trees; excepting one small cluster of apple trees. I think it is too warm throughout the year for the apple tree to produce much fruit; but the others will become abundant.

As to the health of the country, the fact seems to be, that in all the low country, and on the streams of water, the inhabitants are more or less afflicted with the fever and ague. It much resembles Illinois in this particular, as well as in many others. In other situations, I believe it is as healthy as any portion of the United States.

The climate is fine; the air, generally clear and salubrious. It is neither so hot in the summer, or so cold in the winter, as it is in New-England. The country lies between the Gulf of Mexico and the snow-capped Cordillera mountains, so that it is fanned by a refreshing breeze, which ever way the wind may blow.   Sometimes, in winter, the northwest wind sweeps over the plain, strong and keen; and the thin-clad southerner sensibly feels its effects upon his system; and I was informed, instances had been known of their being chilled to death, when obliged to encamp out in the open air without a fire.   It is sometimes cold enough to make thin ice; but, generally, it is mild and pleasant all winter.   The hottest days of summer, are not as warm and oppressive, as we find them at the North.   Individuals originally from Maine and New-Hampshire, said they had found no night so warm, that it was disagreeable to sleep under a woollen blanket.

The rivers are navigable to some extent, whether great or small.   The following are the names of the principal, to wit:—Sabine, Ayish Bayou, Atoyac, Angelina, Neches, Trinity, St. Jacinta, Buffalo Bayou, Navasota, Brazos, Bernard, Canebrake, Colorado, Navedad, La Baca, Guadalupe, San Antonio, Aransaso, Neuces and Rio Grande or Rio del Norte. The streams are all muddy and unpleasant, until you reach the Colorado; this, and those to the south are, generally, clear and beautiful.   About ten miles from the mouth of the Colorado, a raft two miles in extent, obstructs the navigation; when that is removed, boats may go some distance into the country.   The Brazos is navigable at high water, to the falls, about two hundréd and fifty miles from its mouth. A steamboat is now running upon it, as high up as St. Felipe, over a hundred miles.

The Sabine, Neches and Trinity are respectively 350, 300 and 410 miles in length, and are navigable some distance into the country for a considerable portion of the year. The San Bernard is navigable sixty miles. It has 'about four feet of water on the bar at its mouth. The Colorado rises in the high prairies near the mountains, pursues quite a direct course 600 miles and falls into Metagorda Bay.— Above the raft, which is situated ten or twelve miles above its mouth, it is navigable 300 miles. It has as strong a current as that of the Mississippi.

But the Rio del Norte is much the largest and longest river in this region. It rises high up among the mountains, and is estimated to be seventeen hundred miles in length. For two-thirds of its course it runs nearly south; it then changes to the southeast, and empties into the Gulf of. Mexico, near the southern boundary of Texas. It has been ascended by a steamboat two hundred miles to Loredo; and it is stated by those acquainted with the stream, that it is navigable five hundred miles further.

Texas has a seacoast of three hundred and fifty miles; and in a commercial point of view is favorably situated. Its many navigable streams afford great facilities for transporting the rich products of its luxuriant soil to the United States and the rest of the world. It will shortly be settled, its rich lands will become valuable, and it will soon be a great and powerful state.

Mill seats are not plenty. Although the streams run with a lively current, yet there are not many falls suitable for mills ; especially in the lower part of the territory. On the sides of the streams, are occasionally found ledges of limestone ; but none of any kind are seen scattered over the country.— The prairies are free from rocks, brambles, bushes, and every thing except grass. They look like a finely cultivated old field, well set in grass ; sometimes flat, sometimes rolling, but invariably having a surface entirely smooth and unbroken. A carriage can run any where over them. Clay is found all over the country, of an excellent quality for brick. In some places, coal and iron ore are said to have been discovered.

Such are the situation and resources of the country. Let us now look, for a moment, at the inhabitants, and see how they are improved. The Spaniards are not an agricultural people. They are more fond of raising stock, than cultivating the land.— They are also a very social people, and fond of society. They are seldom found on farms alone, and at a distance from neighbors. They formed some small villages in Texas, and left the remainder of the country entirely unsettled. Some ten years ago, the system of grants commenced ; allowing an individual, under certain regulations, to introduce and colonize foreigners. There are now thirteen of these Grants, including a large portion of Texas to wit: Zavala, Burnet and Vehlein—now formed into the Galveston Bay Company—Austin's, Milam's, Robertson's, Cameron's, Dewitt's, De Leon's, Felisola's, McMullen's and McGloin's, Powers' and Beal's. On all these Grants, more or less settlements have been made, and therefore, the population is scattered over an extent of country out of all proportion to their numbers. The large tract granted to each individual, tends to the same result. In riding through regions called settled, a person may not find a house in thirty or forty miles; but generally from ten to twenty miles. I believe there are from forty to fifty thousand inhabitants in Texas; and a large proportion of them are Americans. A person may travel all day; and day after day, and find Americans only. He can hardly make himself believe that he is not still in the United States.

The exports of Texas are cotton, live-stock and peltries. The cotton and peltries are sent either by Natchitoches, or by shipping through the Gulf of Mexico, to New Orleans. The live-stock—cattle, horses and mules, are driven by land across the country to Natchez or New Orleans. The cost of driving is trifling. Plenty of grass is found all the way for the stock; and the drivers carry their provisions, shoot game, &c. and camp down near wood and water by the side of a fire, and cook their meals.

In this manner, a fellow traveller and myself camped out two or three nights. It was quite a novelty to me to sleep in the open air; but the people here think nothing of it. The wolves made rather too much noise, for me to sleep quietly. One night, they awaked me out of a sound sleep, by their discordant yells; I jumped up, dashed a club or two at them, and off they went over the prairies. Our provisions were what they sought, I presume, and not us.

The inhabitants are, many of them, what our northern people would call rather indolent. Occasionally, I found a good farm, large plantation and fine herds of cattle, and all the comforts of life within their dwellings; but more generally, the traveller only finds the log house, built in an open, rude manner, with only one room where he and the family lodge together; and perhaps only corn-bread, meat and sweet potatoes to eat. I called at some places where they had twenty or thirty cows, and could get neither butter, cheese or milk. They let the calves run with the cows, and seldom milk them at all. I did not find butter at half of the places where I called; and obtained cheese only once in Texas. At only three places I found wheat bread.

Although the climate is suitable to the production of Indian corn, yet it is not cultivated to any extent. The reason is, stock is raised with less trouble, and cotton is thought to be a more profitable crop. There is hardly enough corn raised for the consumption of the inhabitants; it, therefore, bears a high price. At St. Felipe, it was a dollar a bushel; and at Velasco on the mouth of the Brazos river, I saw a bushel of shelled corn sold for two dollars!

Thus it is; man seems disinclined to "till the ground," and by "the sweat of his face," to obtain his bread. It often happens, where the earth produces in abundance with little labor, that little is indifferently performed, so that all the comforts and conveniences of life are less enjoyed, than in more sterile soils, and unpropitious climes. Man will, "'mid flowing vineyards die of thirst." Where nature has done almost all, and scattered her favors without stint, man will not stretch forth his hand, and gather her rich bounties. It is not universally so. There are many exceptions to this in Texas. In many instances, the comforts of life are enjoyed there to perfection. Man may not be censured, for not performing severe bodily labor, if he can well provide for himself and those dependant upon him, without it; but life could not have been given, to be spent in listless idleness. A vast field of usefulness is opened to the active man; and he may do much good in his day and generation, other than toil for gain.

But another inducement is held out to the emigrant to settle in Texas, besides the beauty of the country and productiveness of the soil. It is the cheapness of the land. This is no small considera-

tion.   A man with a family obtains a Spanish league
of land, amounting to four thousand four hundred
and twenty-eight English acres, by paying the expense of surveying it, office fees, &c.   These expenses amount to one hundred and eleven dollars,
with the addition of thirty dollars to the government.
So that a man with a family has four thousand four
hundred and twenty-eight acres of land for the small
sum of one hundred and forty-one dollars.   He
must make application to an officer, called an em-
pressario, and obtain his consent; which is given in
the form of a certificate, stating the name of the
family and the quantity of land allowed.   This certificate is presented to another officer, called a com-
missioner, who orders a survey ; and when completed,
makes a deed from the government to the emigrant.
The only condition is, that the land shall be settled
upon, within a limited time.   The emigrant may
make his own selection out of any lands, not previ-
ously granted.   A single man obtains one quarter
of that quantity, with the privilege of having three
quarters more, when he is married.   And provision
is made, that a foreigner, marrying a Mexican woman, may have a league and one third.   These
terms are, certainly, very liberal.   A man here obtains good land, at a cheaper rate, than in any other
part of the world.

But the government have lately adopted another
method of disposing of their land.   A regular land
law has been enacted, and various offices have been

established for the sale of all the vacant land in the province. A person desirous of purchasing public land, goes to the land office in the district where the land is situated, files a petition for a sale, and obtains an order for a survey. This land is laid off into what is called *labors* of one hundred and seventy-seven acres each, and an individual may purchase as many labors as he pleases, up to two hundred and seventy-five, which is about equal to fifty thousand English acres. The minimum price is fixed at ten dollars per labor, the purchaser paying the expense of surveying in addition. One third of the purchase money is payable at the time of sale; the remainder in two equal annual instalments; and the new settlers are exempt from the payment of taxes for the term of ten years.

But Texas has some evils, which will be deemed greater or less, according to the particular section of the country the emigrant may happen to come from. But still, they ought in fairness to be stated, that all may judge for themselves. And in the first place there are three kinds of venomous snakes—the great rattlesnake, the moccason snake, and the prairie rattlesnake. The large rattlesnake is not very plenty, and is seldom seen far out in the open prairie. A gentleman who had lived in the country ten years, told me he had killed only two in the time. The moccason snake, deemed as poisonous as the rattlesnake, seems to be more plenty; but they are not found except in or near wet, marshy land. A gentleman told me, he had a small marsh near his house which seemed to be a haunt for them, as occasionally he found some near it, and in his door yard.— He set half a dozen of his servants to cut down the weeds, and dig a ditch to drain off the water; and in one day they killed *forty-three* moccason snakes; and he pleasantly added, it was not a very good snake day neither. Perhaps this will be set down as another "snake story;" but my authority is Mr Elisha Roberts, living on the main road five miles north of St. Augustine; a very respectable man as I was informed. The prairie rattlesnake is a small one, about a foot in length, similar to that of Illinois. I saw only one in all my wanderings through the country. There are other snakes, not venomous, such as the coach-whip snake, the large black snake, which is here called the "chicken snake," because it sometimes robs hen's nests; the glass snake, which if you strike it, will break in a number of places, and some others. Then, there is the tarantula, which looks like a large brown spider, as big as the palm of the hand; and the stinging lizard, a species of the scorpion, of a reddish color, and about two inches long. The bite of the tarantula and stinging lizard is, in pain and effect, similar to the sting of a bee. There is a weed here, growing all over the country, which is a certain cure for the bite of all these venomous reptiles.

The alligator is found in the rivers of Texas. I saw three, one large one; the other two, small ones.

They sometimes catch hogs, as they go down to the water to drink. They will attack a man in the water. A man was seized by one on Little river, while I was in the country, who was swimming across; but he was beaten off by a person near him, on a raft.

Of the animals, there are many—the panther, wolf, wildcat, tiger cat, bear, Mexican hog, antelope, &c. The wolves are the most numerous, and are quite bold and mischievous. I frequently saw them in the day time, and often heard their discordant howl in the night.

One day, as I was riding along alone in the open woods, a panther came out of a small thicket, into the path before me! I knew that retreat would be dangerous; and, therefore, I boldly sung out and pushed forward towards him. He was not disposed to give battle, but leaped off at once into the woods. I was a good deal startled at this sudden appearance of such a powerful, uncaged beast of the forest; but as he appeared to be the most frightened of the two, I ought to be content. The panther is an animal of the size and color of a full grown lioness, but too cowardly to attack his prey in the open field. Like the Indian, he lies in ambush, or sits perched on the branch of a tree, and seizes his victim unawares. Even a small dog has been known to chase him into his favorite retreat on a tree. The bears, generally, take to the dense forests of trees

13*

and canebrake.   They catch the full grown hogs, and the wolves take the pigs.

Flies, of various kinds, are found here ; and are more troublesome to animals in the warm summer months, than at the north.   I saw large sores, caused by them, on cattle, dogs and hogs.   An application of mercury is sometimes found necessary to cure them.   There is also a wood tick, resembling that on sheep, which fastens itself on animals, but does not appear to do any essential injury.

But last, although not least, in the list of evils, is the ever active moscheto.   In the flat country, bordering on the sea and bays, they are indeed dreadful to a northern man.   When I was at the mouth of the Brazos, towards the last of December, whether on the beach, in the house, on board the vessel, day and night without cessation, the moschetoes were excessively annoying. Give me a general assortment of alligators, snakes and lizards, rather than subject me to the eternal buzz, and stinging bite of the ever busy moscheto.   Other animals may be successfully combatted and subdued ; but to fight the moscheto is like " beating the air ;" give a blow in front and he is in the rear ; brush the rear, and he is in front —and so on all day long.   And when you have done, you have only excessively fatigued and perplexed yourself, and left him the uninjured master of the field. The only chance to get rid of such a keen tormentor as this, is to hang yourself, or run away.

In the high rolling country, there are less flies and no moschetoes.

There are a few remnants of tribes of Indians in the settled region of Texas. They are generally said to be harmless and inoffensive; doing nothing worse than stealing a hog or so, in a neighborly way; so that they may not be entirely forgotten. A woman where I stopped one night, told me that about twenty Indians encamped at the spring near her house; came to the house for meal, and she gave them all she could spare. In the morning, after they were gone, she found they had robbed the yard of all the melons, and taken the fattest shoat she had.

While I was in the country, a man was shot at and wounded by an Indian, near Jones' ferry on the Colorado river. As he was riding along alone over the prairie, he saw a number of Indians by the side of a wood, who beckoned for him to approach. When he had come quite near, happening to cast his eyes towards the wood, he saw an Indian, partly concealed behind a tree, with a gun drawn up in the act of firing. He had only time to throw himself back on his horse, and the ball made a slight flesh wound on his breast. He wheeled, put spurs to his horse and escaped. Whether these were Indians belonging to the settled or unsettled regions of Texas, could not be ascertained.

Between the settlements and the Rocky Mountains, are large tribes of Indians; and detached parties from them, sometimes come down to the border plantations, and steal a few horses. They consider the Spaniards lawful game; but do not care about fighting the Americans. They say, the Americans are a brave people, and fight most desperately; and from them, they obtain their chief supplies.

Perhaps my readers may think this rather a formidable array of animals and reptiles. It may appear more so on paper, and at a distance, than in the region where they are found. People of Mississippi, Alabama and Florida, would find themselves at home among them; but to a northern man they might be found somewhat disagreeable at first.— They would, however, soon become so much accustomed to them, that in a short time they would hardly regard them at all. The inhabitants here, from whatever quarter they may have come, do not think they form any serious objection to settling in the country.

While I remained in Texas, I found no serious trouble from the animals, reptiles or insects, except that general enemy to repose, the moscheto, and that only in the lowlands. On the open prairies, there are but few noxious animals, except the wolves. This is owing a good deal, undoubtedly, to the fire running over them twice a year. As the country becomes more settled, they will be less numerous; and some of them will become entirely extinct.

The water, generally, is very good for a southern country. I found many fine springs of pure soft water in various parts of Texas; and in the rolling prairies, good water is obtained by digging. The only objection to it is in its temperature. To me, it was universally too warm to be agreeable. "A cup of *cold* water" is nowhere to be found in the territory; and to a northern man, in a warm day, it is so refreshing, reviving, invigorating—so readily slakes the thirst, and cools the body, it is almost indispensable to his comfort and enjoyment. Warm water is the common drink of the inhabitants. In the towns, I found the various kinds of spirits and wine; but in the country, I found no spirits, (except very seldom, whiskey) wine, beer, or cider; but only water—*warm water*. It must be admitted, that the people are very temperate, if *not to drink the ardent* be a sure indication of temperance.

There are no large towns in Texas. Bexar, or as it is commonly called, St. Antonio, is the capital, and contains about thirty-five hundred inhabitants—the other villages are small, varying from one hundred to one thousand souls. St. Antonio, like all the Spanish towns, is composed of houses built of logs and mud, and makes a squalid appearance. It is situated about twenty miles east of San Antonio river. The principal towns are, Nacogdoches, St. Augustine; and on Galveston Bay, Harrisburg and Lynchburg: on the Brazos—Velasco, Brazoria, Columbia, St. Felipe, and a new town in Robinson's

colony at the falls : Cole's Settlement, fifteen miles
west of the Brazos: on the Colorado—Metagorda,
Montezuma, Electra, Bastrap, or Mina : on the Gau-
dalupe—Gonsales : on the San Antonio—Goliad,
(formerly Bahia,) and BEXAR : in Powell's Grant—
St. Patrick : on the Rio Grande, or Rio del Norte—
Refugio, Metamoras, Reinosa, Camargo, Mier, Re-
villa, Laredo, Presidio, and the city of Doloros.

A new town is laid out at the falls on the Brazos
river in Robinson's colony, about two hundred and
fifty miles from its mouth. This is the place where
the land office is kept for this colony, and will become quite a village. But the country is not now
settled enough to make or support large towns. It
must be the work of time. Although men may lay
out a town, and commence building it, yet it cannot
prematurely be forced into existence. It must have
a back settlement to support it. The merchant and
mechanic cannot sell, unless there are some inhabitants to buy.

The Spaniards, more than one hundred and fifty
years ago, built some small towns in Texas, the
principal of which are St. Antonio, Nacogdoches and
La Bahia. These became something of villages ;
but for twenty years their population has continually
diminished ; and the country at large does not contain half the Spanish inhabitants that it did at that
time. They, like the Indians, dwindle away, or flee
before the settlements of the Americans.

The Mexican government had three garrisons of soldiers stationed in Texas—one at Nacogdoches, one on Galveston Bay, and one at Velasco, at the mouth of the Brazos. Some of the commanders of these garrisons, attempted to exercise despotic powers, in seizing Americans who had become obnoxious to them, and putting them in prison. About two years ago, their conduct became so oppressive, that the citizens rose *en masse*, killed some of the soldiers, and took the remainder prisoners. The Mexican government then recalled all the officers and soldiers, and there has not been a Mexican garrison in Texas since.

The inhabitants of the country pay no taxes at all. It is said, that the lands are exempt from taxation for ten years to come. All articles imported for the private use of the emigrant, are free of duty; and in fact, a great portion of the merchandize pays none. When I left the Brazos river, there was no custom house officer upon it; and a number of vessel loads of goods were landed, without being required to pay any duty.

Almost all kinds of goods afford a good profit and a ready sale in Texas; especially domestic cottons, boots, shoes, hats and ready made clothing. Coffee is used in large quantities, but I did not find hardly a cup of tea in the whole country. It is not a good place for mechanics. Manufactured articles of all kinds are brought from the north, and sold cheaper than they can be made here; and the country is too thinly settled, and the raw material is too scarce, to give much employment to artisans of what is called custom work, such as shoemakers, tailors, &c. Blacksmiths, however, are an exception to this. They are indispensable, although there are now but few of them. The price charged for shoeing a horse is from three to four dollars.

Texas is connected with Cohahuila, and both form one province of the Mexican Confederacy. But lately, they have been made into separate judicial districts; each having its own courts and officers.— In Texas, their proceedings in court and the records, are in the English language; but land titles are still written in the Spanish. The laws are liberal; they guarantee the freedom of religious opinion and a trial by jury. Courts are held at St. Felipe, Nacogdoches, St. Augustine, Bastrap, &c. The government is elective and republican. I attended an election of sheriff and other county officers. They vote *viva voce*, as the practice is in many of our southern States. To be an inhabitant of the country, is all the qualification necessary to become a voter.

Physicians are occasionally found in the country, and there are a small number of lawyers located in the principal towns. There are but few preachers of the gospel, and I believe no meetinghouses, except some decayed Roman Catholic churches.

The country needs more professional men. It opens a fine field for enterprising men in any profession. The wheels of government in Texas move quietly along. The storms which agitate and distract the city of Mexico and its vicinity, spend their force before they reach that province. I think, the government forms no serious objection to forming a settlement in the country.

But in a new and thinly settled country, the laws, however wise and good, cannot always be enforced. Magistrates and executive officers are few, and courts often at a distance. The new settlers, therefore, sometimes take the law into their own hands ; and although they may not inflict the same punishment the law enjoins, I believe they generally do substantial justice. As an instance of the kind, I will state a case that happened on the bank of the Colorado river. A man settled there, who proved to be a notorious thief. He stole cattle, horses, hogs, or any thing he could lay his hands on. His neighbors resolved to endure his depredations no longer, and gave him notice to depart from that section of the country, or abide the consequences. After waiting awhile, and learning that he intended to remain, some half dozen of his neighbors went to his house in the evening, took him to a tree, and gave him thirty-nine lashes well laid on. They then told him that the punishment should be repeated every week, as long as he remained in the neighborhood. Before a week came round, he left that section of the country and has not been heard of since.

14

In the interior of the country, there is a salt lake, from which a load of fine salt may be obtained in a short time; and appears to be inexhaustible. A small stream runs from this to the Brazos river, and sometimes renders its waters too brackish for use.

By the laws, slavery is not allowed in the province; but this law is evaded by binding the negroes by indenture for a term of years. You will, therefore, find negro servants, more or less, all over the country; but more, on the lowlands, towards the bays and seacoast. Large cotton plantations in this section of the country, are cultivated by negroes; and here also are found some good houses and rich farmers.

Texas lies between the twenty-seventh and thirty-fourth degrees of north latitude; and between sixteen degrees thirty minutes, and twenty-seven degrees west longitude from Washington; and contains probably about one hundred and fifty thousand square miles—as large as all New-England and the State of New-York. It is bounded, east by the Sabine river and a line drawn due north from its head waters to Red River—south, by the Gulf of Mexico—west, by the river Neuces, Rio del Norte, and the Cordillera mountains—north, by the Red River, until it hits its eastern boundary.

More than half of the country is prairie. The margin of the streams and the moist highlands are covered with a fine growth of timber. All the seacoast and on the bays, there is a strip of low, level land, extending seventy miles into the country. The prairies are here very rich, but too level to be pleasant or healthy. The remainder of Texas is high, dry and gently undulating; but not mountainous. Between the rivers Sabine and Trinity, are extensive, gently undulating, sandy plains, generally covered with a good growth of pitch pine ; but occasionally covered with post-oaks, hickory, &c.— Among these, are interspersed small prairies of good land ; sometimes having a black soil, but generally of a reddish cast, and occasionally of a deep red. From the river Trinity to the western line of the State, are high, rolling, beautiful prairies of all sizes and shapes imaginable. So beautiful are these prairies, that the imagination cannot paint a more delightful scene. Cultivation, however nicely performed, will rather mar, than add to their beauty. They are surrounded with a dense forest of trees ; sometimes two or three miles in depth, and sometimes only of a few yards. On the highlands, or elevated plains, are frequently found oak-openings, similar to those of Michigan and Illinois. Texas, with the exception of the pine plains, may with truth be said to possess a deep, rich soil of black marl.

That portion of the country lying between the Colorado river and Louisiana, is subject to powerful rains in the fall and spring ; but as you go southward and westward towards the city of Mexico, the rains become less frequent, and not so abundant.—

About two months in summer, it is generally quite dry ; sometimes, so severe is the drought that vegetation withers, and the grass on the prairies becomes dry. To the southward of Texas, the Spaniards irrigate their lands to make them produce a more abundant crop. The planting season is so early, (from the first to the middle of February,) that all the crops, except cotton and sugar cane, come to maturity before the dry weather commences ; and these get such a vigorous start in this luxuriant soil, that they are seldom materially injured by the drought.

The roads are all in a state of nature ; yet so smooth is the surface, and so gently undulating is the face of the country, that in dry weather, better roads are not found any where. A person, however, often meets with moist bottom land, and streams difficult to pass. In the wet season, travelling is more disagreeable and difficult ; and sometimes, impracticable, on account of the swollen, rapid streams of water.

Although carriages run without difficulty all over the country, yet the inhabitants have not yet introduced pleasure carriages. The mode of travelling is on horseback ; but women and children often go in a baggage wagon drawn by oxen. Baggage wagons are quite numerous, but I found only one pleasure carriage in the whole province, and that was a gig-wagon.

Emigrants are continually pouring into Texas, both by sea and land, and from every section of the United States. The southerners generally choose the lowlands bordering on the bays and Gulf; but the northern people prefer the high lands in the interior. If emigration continues, it will soon contain a very respectable population.

I found some of the emigrants disappointed, discontented and unhappy; and I met one man on his return to the land from whence he came. He was from Tennessee, had moved into Texas with his family and a small portion of his goods in a wagon; but they all did not like the country so well as the one they had left, and unanimously agreed to return. It was a tedious and expensive journey, but not altogether useless. It will teach them more highly to prize their own country, neighborhood and privileges, and induce them to spend the remainder of their days with contented minds.

Before a man with a family makes up his mind to emigrate to a new, unsettled and distant country, he ought well to consider of the subject. Emigration, like matrimony, ought to be fully considered; as a bad move in this particular, is attended by many evils, and cannot well be remedied. In the first place, it is the best way to "let well enough alone." If an individual be well settled in life, has profitable employment, well supports himself and family and gains a little every year, dwells in an agreeable neighborhood, has the privilege of sending his chil-
14*

dren to school, and of attending public worship, why should he wish to remove? Why should he wish to go into the wilderness, endure the fatigues of a long journey, and the many hardships and deprivations necessarily attendant upon a removal to the most favored spot in the new world? This life is too short and uncertain to be spent in making doubtful experiments. It is wise, to live where we can be the most useful and happy ourselves, and where we have the fairest prospect of rendering others so, with whom we are connected.

But the young man, who has no lucrative employment, and the married man who has to labor hard to gain a scanty subsistence for himself and family, would do well to go to the rich prairies of the south or west. He ought to be careful not to be too much elated with the prospect before him, for disappointment, fatigue and suffering most assuredly await him. It is not "a light thing" to travel with a family and goods two or three thousand miles.— He ought to accustom his mind to dwell upon hardship and suffering, before he commences his journey. Young says :—

" Our only lesson is to learn to suffer;
" And he who knows not that, was born for nothing."

But on his arrival at his location in the new world, however fine, rich and elegant the situation may be, he will feel disappointed and sad. This is perfectly natural; and although some may have too much

pride to acknowledge it, yet they all have a strange-
ness of feeling pervading their breasts, that is sometimes painful in the extreme. Perhaps the emigrant
had never before travelled far from the smoke of his
father's dwelling, and had spent his life hitherto in
the neighborhood where he was born, and where his
early and innocent attachments were formed. He
now finds himself in a new country, far away from
the ever-to-be-remembered scenes of his childhood,
and he looks abroad upon the world around him, in
sadness of heart; for it is a world, however beautiful it may be, that is a stranger to him, and with
which he has no sympathy. Not to feel, under
such circumstances as these, indicates something
more or less than man. And this strange, lonely
feeling, is hardly softened down and mitigated,
by the well known fact, that his new location is far
superior to the one he has left. The inhabitants of
Nantucket are proverbially attached to that island
of sand, and are discontented and unhappy in the
most fertile towns and beautiful villages on the continent.

The emigrant ought to think of all these things,
before he leaves his native village. But when he
has become located in the new world, it will not do
to shrink back and despond. He must brace himself to the task before him, and cheer up his family,
who in fact need some cheering, for exchanging a
well built house and pleasant associates, for the rude
log hut and wild beasts of the forest. They will all

soon become acquainted with the new world and form new associations. A well built house will shortly take the place of the rude cabin, and emigrants will settle near them, to whom they will become attached. The rich fields will produce an abundant harvest, and large flocks of cattle will be seen feeding on the luxuriant grass. He will soon gain a competeney, live at ease, and become contented and happy.

The inhabitants have a strong belief that Texas will at some future day become one of the United States ; but I think this, extremely doubtful. It is more probable, that it will in time become an independent sovereignty. It is now one of the Mexican States, and the seat of the general government is the city of Mexico. The confederacy is composed of quite a number of States, and Texas sends its due proportion of representatives to the general Congress, to make laws for the whole. These States have never been well agreed in their form of government, or in the men for rulers. Revolutions, and counter-revolutions, have been the order of the day at the seat of the general government; but Texas is too much settled by Americans, and is too far removed from these intestine commotions to be much affected by them.

Col. Stephen F. Austin, to whom the first colony was granted, and who has been the indefatigable pioneer in the settlement of Texas, has generally been its representative in the general government.—

In the spring of 1834, he was at the seat of government, but so great were the divisions that little business could be done. He considered the country in a state of revolution, and wrote home to a friend of his, that he believed Texas had better take care of itself and form a government of its own. This friend proved treacherous, enclosed his letter to the President, and sent it to the city of Mexico. It was received just after Col. Austin had left the city on his return home. He was pursued, arrested, brought back and put in prison. He was for awhile kept in close confinement; and then, let out on his giving bonds to confine himself to the limits of the city. When I was in Texas, it was believed, he would shortly be liberated, and was daily expected home; but I have since learned, that he is still retained a prisoner.

It requires not the gift of prophecy to tell what the end of these things will be. Texas will become tired of belonging to such a discordant confederacy; and when their population shall have sufficiently increased to insure success, will throw off the yoke and form a government of their own. But at all events it will soon be disjoined from Cohahuila, establish its own State government and elect its own officers. The seat of government will probably be San Felipe, on the Brazos river.

In some publications the people of Texas have been slandered. They have been called a set of robbers and murderers, screening themselves from justice, by fleeing from their own country and coming to this. It would be strange indeed, if there were not such instances; but whoever travels over the country, will find them as pleasant, obliging and kind as any people in the United States. In the towns, you generally find a billiard room; and near it, a race-course. At these resorts, are found the favorite amusements of the inhabitants. I went all through the country, unarmed and unharmed; nor did I at any time fall in jeopardy of life or limb.— Their most prominent fault is, in being too fond of pastime and hunting, to the neglect of tilling the land, building decent houses, and procuring the conveniences of life.

The most healthy and pleasant portions of Texas are in the regions of Nacogdoches; in the rolling country between the Brazos and Colorado; and southward and westward of the latter river—in Beal's Grant near the Rio del Norte; and high up on the Brazos and its branches, in Robinson's colony. But neither Galveston Bay, nor the flat country all along the seacoast, is the place for a northern man. It is too much infested with alligators, moccason snakes and moschetoes. It is more suitable for southern planters, to be cultivated by the blacks.

But whoever emigrates with his family to Texas, let him at all events, carry with him bread stuffs to last six months; for there is no wheat raised in the country, and only a small crop of corn for the supply of its own inhabitants. Of course, bread stuffs are always dear, and sometimes unattainable at any price. Cattle and hogs are plenty, and wild game abundant, so that he could supply himself with meat in this country.

The emigrant had better buy his cattle and horses here; for those brought from a more northern climate, do not thrive well, and often die. A good servicable horse may be bought for, from twenty to thirty dollars; a cow with a calf by her side, for ten dollars; and a yoke of oxen, for about thirty dollars. The land is ploughed by oxen, horses and mules; but journeys for the transportation of merchandize are performed by oxen.

There is a mail running from the city of Mexico, through St. Felipe, as far as Nacogdoches; but as the United States mail goes no farther than fort Jessup, the two mails do not meet each other, by seventy-five miles. There is, therefore, no mail connection between the United States and Texas. This is a serious inconvenience, and must shortly be remedied. The only chance to send a letter either way, is by a private conveyance. This is generally done by the captains of vessels.

The currency is silver and gold coin, bills of the United States Bank and those of New Orleans.— Copper coins are not found in circulation at the south and west. Texas has no bank of its own.

Thus much for my general view of Texas. I have endeavored to give a true account of the country as it appeared to me. Perhaps it may not be altogether acceptable to landholders and speculators. Be that as it may, I believe I have performed an acceptable service to the emigrant, by giving him a fair account of the country; and one that he will find to be a true one, in all its essential particulars, on his arrival. Live stock, cotton and sugar are and will be the great staples of the country—grain will be of secondary consideration.

What, then, is the conclusion of the whole matter? Is Texas a desirable place for a northern man? My opinion is, that if a northern man would locate himself in the highlands of the country, he would enjoy health as well as at the north; procure all the necessaries and conveniences of life much easier; and might in time, become independently rich. I do think, he would find the climate more pleasant, and more congenial to his feelings, than a northern one; and his life probably attended by more enjoyments.

I have been frequently asked, what particular spot in Texas is the most desirable, for an emigrant to settle in? My answer is, I cannot tell. And whoever travels over the country, will be as much puzzled to tell, as I am. The fact is, there are hundreds of places offering about the same inducements—all pleasant, healthy and agreeable. Among them, it is quite immaterial what particular one the emigrant may select. I saw an emigrant who had been in the country almost a year, and he had been

riding over it, the chief part of the time, and still
was unable to make a selection. He said, there
were so many fine situations, so nearly alike, that he
found it difficult to give a decided preference to any
particular one. When he will be able to make up
his mind, and decide the question, I know not.—
The last time I saw him, he was still on the wing;
and for aught I know, he may keep in motion, as
long as the far-famed Boston traveller, *Peter Rugg*,
or the *Flying Dutchman*, and never be able to find
a spot of ground for a permanent abode! But this
emigrant is not to be " sneezed at." Questions of
far less importance have agitated the world ; and
who knows, but that the destiny of the country, as
well as his own, eminently depends upon his particular location!

Again—I have been enquired of, what can a man
do to make property in Texas? I answer, he can
go into trade in some of the villages and make large
profits upon his goods. He can go on to a plantation and raise cotton, sugar, corn or stock—any or
all of these are easily raised and find a ready market. This is what he *may* do ; but what he *will* do,
is altogether uncertain. He may become as indolent
and inattentive to business, as many of the inhabitants of the country. He may spend his time in
hunting, at the race-course, and at the billiard table.
Here, at the north, the great anxiety is, how we
shall live—wherewithal we shall be clothed, and
how we can turn a penny to " get gain ;" *there*, the

15

great concern is, how they shall employ themselves
to kill time. *Here*, we struggle hard to live; *there*,
they strive hard not to live. *Here*, we live in spite
of nature; *there*, nature makes them live in spite of
themselves. Could an emigrant know what course
he would take on settling in Texas, he could then
tell, whether it would be better to go or remain. I
have spread the country open before him; let him
judge for himself. And fortunate is he, who gives
heed to the experience of others, and makes a wise
choice.

I concluded to return to the north by water. I
procured a conveyance from the interior to St. Felipe on horseback; and here, I learnt that there was
a schooner sixty miles down the river at Columbia,
bound to New Orleans, which would sail in a few
days. I could find no conveyance to Columbia,
either by land or water. I found a wagon going
down for merchandize, on which I put my baggage;
and in company with another gentleman, whom I
found in the same predicament with myself, started
off on foot.

St. Felipe is the head quarters of Austin's colony.
It is a small village, on a high prairie, immediately
on the south bank of the Brazos river, nearly one
hundred miles from the sea. It stands on the first
high land you come to on the river; and at this spot
the high rolling country commences. Its situation
is beautiful and commanding. It has two taverns,
four or five stores, a court house, and perhaps twen-

ty dwelling houses; but there are only two or three good looking buildings in the place. The opposite side of the river is low and covered with a heavy growth of timber.

St. Felipe, like most of the southern villages, is not without its billiard room; and its usual, I might say invariable accompaniment, the grog shop.— Billiards is a pleasant and manly game enough; and good exercise for a sedentary man; and if indulged in only for amusement, is as innocent as any recreation whatever. It is a game much played in the middle and southern portions of the United States; and men of the first respectability are found at the table. But in this section of the country, it cannot be recommended as a safe place for recreation. It is generally used as a mere gambling apparatus; and a person meets with a class of society not the most civil, sober and peaceable.

Not long since, a young man played with an old gambler, until he became tired, and started off. The gambler came out at the door, and called him back; but finding he could not induce him to return, out of mere wantonness and sport, commenced throwing brickbats at him. The young man was a cripple, and could neither run, or successfully contend with his athletic opponent. He bore it as long as he could, then drew a pistol and shot him through the body. He fell dead upon the spot, without uttering a word. He had been an overbearing, troublesome fellow, and his death was the cause of joy rather than sorrow.

One night, while I was at St. Felipe, two young men returned from a bloody affray, thirty miles down the river. Early the next morning, two other men, fully armed, entered the town in pursuit, and paraded the streets in hostile array. I enquired into the history of the case, and found the following particulars.

Some time previous, one of the young men paid his addresses to a young lady, and was engaged to be married. He went to the north on some mercantile business; and during his absence, another young man by the name of Thompson, commenced his particular attentions to the young lady; and the match was strongly advocated by his father. On his return from the north, he and another young man who had married a sister of the lady in question, payed a visit to her father's—stayed all night, and started in the forenoon, to return to St. Felipe.— One of them was in a light gig-wagon, the other on horseback. They had proceeded but a few miles when they heard the clattering of horses' feet, at full speed, behind them. On looking round, they saw young Thompson's father, and a doctor of the neighborhood, in close pursuit, with pistols in hand. The young men were also armed; and immediately shots were exchanged by both parties. But such was the hurry and agitation of the moment, that none took effect. They all dismounted at once, and at it they went, in a desperate contest for life and death. The doctor, not liking this part of the game, or not feeling exactly brave on the occasion, was contented to stand aloof, and see the battle rage. Old Thompson was a powerful man, and about an equal match for both of his opponents. He laid about him like a giant; and sometimes had one grounded, and then the other; and apparently, would shortly gain the victory over them both. At length, he knocked one down, and seemed determined to despatch him at once. He seized him by the throat, and called upon the doctor for a knife. The other young man saw at a glance the critical state of the contest—he jumped to the wagon, took out a loaded gun, just in time to stop the doctor, by his threats, from handing the knife, then took deliberate aim at Thompson, and shot him through the body. Thompson fell back, said he was a dead man, and expired in a few minutes. The doctor ran to his horse, mounted and fled with all convenient speed. The young men, having been rather roughly handled, were considerably bruised, although not seriously injured. They picked up the deadly weapons of the battle-field, as trophies of victory, and made the best of their way to St. Felipe.

In a short time, the doctor, young Thompson and some others, came to the battle-ground, and carried home the dead body; and without waiting to attend the funeral, young Thompson and the doctor started after the young men, to avenge his death. It

15*

caused no small stir at St. Felipe, when they arrived, and paraded the streets fully armed, and breathing out threatenings. The young men took to a store, and with arms in their hands, awaited the result.— The civil authority, however, interfered. The young men gave themselves up to the custody of the law, and Thompson and the doctor were persuaded to go home, and abide a trial by jury.

It is no pleasure to me to give an account of such lawless battles; but as a faithful chronicler of events I could not pass·them over in silence. Texas, however, is not more the theatre of them, than many places in the United States. If the value of an article is enhanced in proportion to its scarcity, it is more excusable to fight for a lady here, than elsewhere; for, according to the best estimate I could make, there are ten men to one woman in the country. And could the surplus maiden population of New-England be induced to emigrate to Texas, they would meet with a cordial reception; and it might prove, not only advantageous to themselves, but highly beneficial to the country.

In two miles from the town, we came to the flat, low country. It was, generally, muddy and very disagreeable and fatiguing to travel over. It was all an open prairie country, except a small skirt of timber immediately on the banks of the little streams; and almost a dead level, except in one place, twelve miles from Columbia. Here, a hundred acres or more rise thirty or forty feet above the general level of the country, and by way of distinction, is called " the mound." Near the streams, the ground was a little elevated; and at such places, we found houses, and some small improvements, probably, in eight or ten miles of each other. We saw a great many herds of deer, and flocks of wild geese and ducks.

We were almost four days in performing the route; and were excessively fatigued, when we entered the small village of Columbia. This is a new village, having two or three stores, a tavern, and half a dozen dwelling houses. It is situated on a level prairie, two miles from the river, and ten above Brazoria. There is a small village immediately on the bank of the river, called Bell's Landing; and the space between the two, is low bottom land, heavily covered with timber.

At this landing, vessels come up and unload their merchandize, destined for the upper country. It has a tavern, two stores, a large warehouse, and three or four dwelling houses. Here I was informed, the schooner had dropped down the stream. I stopped over night, and rather than walk, I obtained a log canoe, and a man to paddle me down to Brazoria. The tide sets up a little further than Bell's Landing, and our boat, having the advantage of its ebb and the current also, floated us down in two hours.

Brazoria is quite a large village. I found some very good buildings, public houses, stores, and as

usual, a billiard room. A newspaper is published
here, called the Brazoria Gazette; and I believe is
the only one printed in all Texas. The situation of
the town is low and unpleasant ; and subject to the
fever and ague. I found a steamboat here, going
up the river; but the vessel had gone further down ;
so we started in the canoe after her; and rowing
fifteen miles we found her by the side of the river,
taking in bales of cotton. I was glad to get on
board the vessel, and be relieved at once from the
tediousness and fatigue of pursuit, and from the uncertainty of obtaining a passage to the United
States.

The vessel remained here, until the next day,
when we sailed with a light breeze down the stream.
The river is very crooked, so that it is twice as far
from Brazoria to its mouth by water, as it is by land.
We had to tie the vessel up to a tree at night, as it
was too dark to proceed. The next day in the
afternoon, we hauled up again, on account of a head
wind. The mate stept ashore to spend the time in
hunting. The river is lined with timber on both
sides, about a mile in width ; and then, the country
is generally an open, level prairie. The mate became entirely bewildered and lost; could not find
his way back to the vessel ; and was obliged to
camp out for the night. In the morning, the captain sent scouts in various directions after him ; but
they all returned without success. The captain concluded he must have gone towards the mouth of the

river; so he hoisted sail and started on. Nearly noon, the mate made his appearance on the river bank, nearly opposite the vessel; and the captain sent his boat for him. He was quite exhausted.— He had wandered about almost the whole time, and could neither find a house, road or river. He said he never had been used to hunting; but he could not conceive why people were so fond of it, as it was much more pain than pleasure to him. 'Every one to his trade.' A hunter would have found as little pleasure on the ocean, as the sailor did on the land. This hunting expedition afforded no little merriment to the captain and crew, at his expense, during the voyage.

The timber on the river banks became less, as we descended; and for five miles above the mouth, there is none at all. A small town called Velasco is situated on the sandy beach, at the river's mouth— containing one public house, two stores, four or five dwelling houses, and the ruins of an old Spanish fort. We stayed two days here, waiting for a fair wind to cross the bar. I frequently amused myself by walking for miles on the sandy beach, and picking up some of the pretty shells among the millions that lay scattered along. It is as fine a walk as a pensive maiden, in contemplative mood, could desire. On the one hand, is the ever-toiling ocean, whose waves break upon the sand bars, and in giddy globes of foam, lash the shore, and spend their force beneath your feet; on the other, a low, sandy bluff, and then an extended lawn, stretching far away into the interior, and its utmost verge skirted with stately forest trees; and the pathway itself, smooth, hard and level, and bedecked with countless beautiful shells of various sizes, shapes and hues.

The Brazos is an unpleasant stream. Its waters are at all times muddy; its banks are generally low and present a raw edge to the eye as you pass along; and in many places the navigation is rendered difficult, by reason of the many snags. At its mouth, there is a bar, generally having not more than five or six feet of water; and the channel so narrow that a vessel can only pass through with a fair wind. Three vessels had been wrecked on the coast the past season. The remains of two of them, lay in sight partly buried in the sand.

In the spring, the waters of all the streams in Texas are high, and bring down from the upper country, large quantities of timber. The mouth of the Brazos, and a long distance on the seashore, is lined with large masses of trees; and from this source the inhabitants of Velasco obtain their fuel.

One morning, near the last of December, the captain announced a fair wind. He weighed anchor, hoisted sail, and with a stiff breeze pushed out to sea. The vessel only drew five feet water, yet she touched three or four times on the bar; but did no apparent damage. I stood upon the deck, until the land, trees and houses faded away in the distance.

Texas, like a beautiful damsel, has many charms
and attractions, but is not entirely faultless. Indeed,
there is no such place as a perfect elysium on earth.
And those who have formed their opinion of the
country from some of the many late publications
concerning it, will feel some disappointment on their
arrival. But its many beauties will hide a multitude
of faults ; or render them light and easily borne. I
must say of Texas, as Cowper said of England,
" with all its faults, I like it still ;" and although I
had experienced some hardships and inconveniences
while in the country, yet its mild climate, pleasant
streams, and enchanting " fields of living green," I
left at last with serious regret.

The fall of the year is the best time to move into
Texas ; or into any of the western States. There
are four good reasons to give for this preference :
1st. It is then better travelling ; both on account of
the dryness of the roads, and the mild temperament
of the weather—neither too hot or too cold. 2d. It
is more healthy on the road—not so much danger
of contracting disease on the way ; and to be there
at the opening of the spring, and become accustomed to the climate and warm weather by degrees,
there will be a fairer prospect of continued health.
3d. It is the time of the year when provisions are
the most plenty and cheapest ; an emigrant can,
therefore, the more readily supply himself on the
road, and after his arrival. 4th. It is the shortest
time a person can be in the country, and raise a

crop the ensuing season. To arrive in October, or the first of November, he will have plenty of time to build a log house, split out rails and fence in a field by the coming spring, so as to raise a crop.— Were he to go in the spring, he would be obliged to support himself and family a whole year before he could get a crop into the ground.

To go from the north to Texas, the better way is to take a passage on board a vessel bound to Galveston Bay, the river Brazos, or the Colorado. But if a vessel cannot readily be found, going direct to Texas, a passage may be taken to New Orleans; and from thence, a person can go up the Red River to Natchitoches, and across the country; or by water through the Gulf, to almost any port on the bays and rivers. The distance from Boston by water, is three thousand miles; by land, it is not quite so far. From the city of New-York, vessels frequently may be found going direct to Texas. The most convenient places for landing in Texas are Harrisburg, on Galveston Bay; Velasco, at the mouth of the Brazos, and Metagorda at the mouth of the Colorado. It would be advisable to get a protection, more especially, if a person goes by water.

Speculation—ever busy, active speculation, pervades the world. It rages with violence in Maine, disturbs the quiet villages of New-England, keeps the western world alive, and visits the shores of Texas. I was at a loss to know how speculation could get hold of Texas lands; for they are only granted to the actual settler; and only one grant given to each. Human ingenuity has devised a plan. When an emigrant arrives in the country, he is met by a land speculator, who tells him he knows of a good location, and if he will go and settle on it, he shall have one half of the league for nothing. The land is entered at the land office in the emigrant's name, the speculator pays the fees, and takes a deed of one half, from the emigrant. This is not the worst kind of speculation in the world. It probably may prove beneficial to both parties. The emigrant at least, seems to have no cause for complaint. He gets twenty-three hundred acres of land, as much as he can ever cultivate, and pays nothing at all for it.

We had four passengers on board; two of whom were afflicted with that lingering disease called the fever and ague. They had resided a few months in the lowlands of Texas, and became so severely afflicted, they were returning to the United States for health. The other was a physician, who had gone up the river as far as Columbia; did not like the country, and was on his return home to Tennessee. I informed him, he had not seen the most desirable portion of the country. And such was the fact.— But he had read some of the descriptions of the " beautiful river Brazos and the fine country adjacent," and was thereby completely deceived.

A sea voyage is always unpleasant to me. The wind blew a strong breeze, the waves rolled high,

16

and made our vessel dance over them like a feather. We all became dreadfully sea sick. It is a terrible feeling ; and those afflicted with it, probably endure as much excruciating pain and distress, as the human system is capable of sustaining. In two days, the wind abated in a measure, and the sea became comparatively smooth. We crawled out upon deck, our sickness abated, and soon left us entirely.

On the fifth day, just at night, we saw the light at the southwest pass of the Mississippi. It soon became dark, and the captain in attempting to enter the mouth of the river, run the vessel aground near the shore. A scene here occurred, that somewhat startled us. We were in the cabin and felt the vessel strike, and heard the waves dash against her.— We ran up on deck, and there saw the captain seated upon the windlass, writhing in agony, and groaning like one in despair ! The idea struck us in a moment, that the captain saw our danger to be iminent, the vessel would dash in pieces, and we must all perish. But we were immediately relieved from our apprehensions. In the darkness of the night, and hurry of the moment, the captain had been thrown across the pump, and severely injured ; and it was from actual pain of body, rather than anguish of mind, that made him groan so bitterly. We did not, however, feel entirely at ease. We were exposed to the open sea ; and if the wind should rise, and blow hard on shore, the vessel must be dashed to pieces, and we escape the best way we could.

But we were highly favored. The wind died
away and the sea became quite calm. We retired
to our berths, and slept quietly. In the morning,
we carried out an anchor; at flood tide, hauled the
vessel off ; a steamboat took us in tow, and at the
dinner hour, we were gallantly gliding up the river.
So change the scenes of life.

The Mississippi steam tow-boats have engines of
immense power. Our boat had six vessels in tow,
and it carried us along at the rate of four miles an
hour, against the strong current of the river. From
the mouth of the Mississippi to New Orleans is one
hundred and fifteen miles, and we performed the
trip in about twenty-eight hours. The price charged for towing up the river is a dollar a ton ; and the
amount the boat received from all the vessels, was
about five hundred dollars. The vessels are towed
down stream for half price, and sometimes less.

Fifteen miles from the sea, the Mississippi divides
itself into three channels, each having a lighthouse,
near the mouth ; but the southwest pass is the only
one in which ships can enter when loaded. The
river continually pushes its banks further out to sea.
They are formed of mud and logs, and soon become
covered with a rank growth of rushes.

The banks of the river are low, and too wet for
cultivation, for fifty miles from the sea. Soon after
passing fort Jackson, which is about forty miles up
the river, we came to sugar plantations on both
sides, and these continued to the city of New Or-

leans.. On many of these large plantations we saw
elegant houses, surrounded by orange trees, loaded
with fruit. In the rear, sugar houses and steam
mills for grinding the cane, and long rows of neat
looking negro houses; and large stacks of rice
standing near them. The planters were all busily
engaged in making sugar; and we saw armies of
negroes in the fields, cutting and transporting the
cane to the mills. January had already commenced,
yet there had been no frost to destroy vegetation,
and the cane looked as green as in midsummer.—
The crop of sugar was unusually large, and of an
excellent quality.

The sugar cane, in size, stalk and leaf, very much
resembles the southern corn. It has, however, no
spindles at the top, like the corn stalk, but terminates in a tuft of long leaves. It does not appear
to produce any seed in this country; but the crop is
annually renewed, by planting short slips of the
stalk. Its juice is sweet, pleasant and nutritious.
The negroes are very fond of chewing the stalk; and
I saw some bundles of it at the vegetable market in
New Orleans for sale. When the cane comes to
maturity, it is cut up and ground with smooth nuts,
which in fact only compress the stalk, and force out
the juice. This is caught in a large trough underneath, and undergoes the same process of boiling in
large kettles, as the sap of a northern maple, when
made into sugar. When the boiling is completed,
the sugar is put into a large cistern full of holes in

the bottom, where it remains a number of days, that all the molasses that will, may drain out. It is then put into hogsheads, and sent to market.

On the eastern bank of the Mississippi, stands the city of New Orleans. It is regularly laid out, chiefly built of brick, has many fine blocks of buildings, large houses, and handsome streets ; but its site is too low for it to appear to advantage, or to render it pleasant and agreeable. It stretches two miles along the river bank ; and for that distance, the levee is lined with triple and quadruple rows of vessels, steamboats and flat-boats ; all having their particular location by themselves. The trade of New Orleans is immense. By the weekly shipping register, it appeared there were two hundred and thirty-four vessels in port. The levee is loaded with bales of cotton, barrels of pork and flour, hogsheads of hams, kegs of lard, and hogsheads of sugar and molasses. It is a place of great business, bustle and blandishment ; and of dissipation, disease and death.

As I passed along by its muddy pavements and putrid gutters, and saw the many gambling houses, grog shops, oyster shops, and houses of riot and debauchery, surely, thought I, there are many things here exceedingly offensive, both to the physical and moral man. And when I saw the motley throngs, hurrying on to these haunts of vice, corruption and crime, I almost instinctively exclaimed, in the words of the immortal bard—

"Broad is the road that leads to death,
"And thousands walk together there!"

16*

But here, the career of the debauchee is short. The poisonous atmosphere soon withers and wastes away his polluted life's blood. Death follows close upon the heels of crime; and one need stand but a short time at the charnel-house, to behold cartloads of his victims, hurried on, " unwept, unhonored and unsung," to their last home!

Life seems to be valued by its possessor, in proportion to the strength of the tenure by which it is held. When danger becomes imminent, and life's termination apparently near, instead of making the most of its short duration, man improvidently throws it away, as of no value; or suppresses all apprehension of the future, by rushing headlong into the wildest excesses of dissipation and crime. This is sometimes exemplified in the sailor. When perils thicken around, and death stares him in the face, instead of summoning all his powers into action, and bravely contending to the last, he attempts to shut his eyes upon impending ruin, by stupifying the body, and ignobly surrenders life without a struggle. On no other principle, can I account for the excesses of New Orleans. In its best estate, it is emphatically a place of disease and death. Its atmosphere is pestiferous. It is felt so to be, and so considered by its citizens. One might suppose, amid the ravages of disease and death, a man would think seriously and live soberly. That if his days were to be very few, he would make them all count, and tell to the greatest advantage. But the inhabitants of New

Orleans, instead of attempting to deprive death of his power, are enlisted on his side—they put poisoned arrows in his quiver, and add new terrors to his name! The sanctions of law and religion are set at nought, the Sabbath profaned, and they give themselves up to hilarity, dissipation and crime. Is this denied? The fact is too apparent and notorious, successfully to be concealed or denied. Could the many victims of debauchery and crime speak, they might "unfold a tale" that would cause "the hair of the flesh to stand up," and make the boldest turn pale. Shall I be asked to particularize? Take the Criminal Code, and there read its long list of enormities and crimes.

Censures are painful, and comparisons are deemed invidious; but I must say, New Orleans does not show that order, neatness and sobriety, found in other large cities of the Union. Murders, robberies, thefts and riots, are too common hardly to elicit a passing notice. Man here seems to have become reckless of life. It is taken and given for "trifles light as air," with an indifference truly astonishing. The police is inefficient, or shamefully negligent.— The authorities of the city appear to stand aloof, and see the populace physically and morally wallowing in the mire. It does appear to me, that if all in authority, and all the virtuous portion of the citizens would brace themselves to the work, the city might be greatly improved in health and in morals. Let the strong arm of the law be put forth fearlessly—let the streets be cleared of the mud and filth, the gutters of their putrid water—let the police be active and take into custody the disorderly knaves and vagabonds—let gambling houses be put down, and Sunday theatres and circuses be suppressed, and New Orleans would wear a different aspect.— Then, might its streets be walked without fear of life or limb; and the great wealth flowing in, by canal, railroad and river, be fully enjoyed.

This may be thought by some to be an exaggerated account of the city. For the honor of our country and of human nature, I wish it might be. But it is, indeed, too true ; and whoever happens to visit it, that places a decent value upon life, or the goods of this life, will be glad, like me, to escape without the injury or loss of either. Although the vessel I came in was robbed of money and wearing apparel ; one of its sailors, knocked down and his money taken from him ; and a companion of mine had his pocket book cut from his pocket; yet, I fortunately escaped. I could not, however, feel at ease among such a set of plunderers and robbers.

I am fully aware, that a large portion of the populace is made up of all nations, tongues and languages ; that their residence here, is often transient ; that many enormities are incidental to all large cities of such a mixed population ; and that the many worthy citizens ought not to be held responsible for all the crimes that may be committed, unless they make themselves accessory to them, by indifferently

looking on, and taking no energetic measures to prevent them. But it does appear to me, they are cul-
pably negligent in this particular.

The city authorities need not sanction crime, by
licensing gambling houses and houses of ill-fame.
By so doing, they take from themselves the power
of frowning upon crime, or of effectually punishing
the criminal; but leave him to assume an unblush-
ing boldness in society, not elsewhere witnessed,
that is truly alarming. If crime may not be entirely prevented, it can be rendered disgraceful; and
those who have a decent respect for the opinion of
mankind, if they have none for themselves, will then
be deterred from committing evil. But as long as
New Orleans is believed to be a place, where crimes
may be committed with impunity, and without incurring the censure or disapprobation of its citizens ;
so long will it be the general haunt for the knaves
and vagabonds of the Union, and of the world.—
They will centre here; give countenance and support to each other; draw within their deadly grasp
the unsuspecting, the vicious and the idle; and, like
the rolling snow-ball, at every impulse enlarge their
circle, and gain additional force and power.

It is time, high time for all the sober minded and
well disposed to awake, look about them, and see
their true condition. Theirs is the sleep of death.
Like Jonah of old, they slumber amid the whirlwind
and storm. New Orleans needs reform; and in a

righteous cause, small means may effect much. Ten
men may chase a thousand. Can the result be
doubtful?

> ————" Our doubts are traitors;
> And make us lose the good we oft might win,
> By fearing to attempt."

But I have done with the health and moral condition of New Orleans. I am told it has improved,
and is improving. And yet there is room—an ample field for the philanthropist to exercise the utmost
stretch of his powers, to improve the physical and
moral condition of its citizens.

A particular description of the city is not necessary. Its favorable location for foreign and domestic trade, and vast resources, are well known. One
thing was new to me. It contains about half a doz-
en large cotton presses, entirely occupied in compressing bales of cotton. Those intended for a foreign market, are made to occupy one half of their
original space; so that a vessel can carry double the
quantity it otherwise might. The large number of
bales shipped from this port, makes this an extensive business. The charge for compressing is seventy-five cents a bale. Bales designed for the northern ports, do not undergo this operation, but are shipped as they come from the hands of the planter.

New Orleans has three extensive markets; two
for flesh, and one for vegetables. I walked through
them all, and thought the city was abundantly supplied with provisions, and of a good quality. Al-

though it was January, the vegetable market was supplied with melons, green peas, radishes, lettuce, &c. And boats frequently landed, with cart loads of oranges, fresh from the trees. Fish are neither abundant, or of a fine flavor.

On the opposite side of the river, are the ship-yards; but they seem to be more occupied in repairs, than in building new vessels. Here is a small village of a dozen houses, a grog shop and a tavern. A steam ferry boat constantly plies across the river, and appears to have a plenty of business.

The city is connected with lake Pontchartrain, by a canal for small vessels, and a railroad. The distance is five miles. Steamboats regularly run from the end of the railroad, to Mobile and other ports. New Orleans has no wharves. It would be more convenient in loading vessels to have them; but they cannot be built on a foundation sufficiently firm to withstand the strong current of the Mississippi. A few years ago a wharf was built; but it was soon undermined and sunk in the stream.

After remaining in the city four days, I procured a passage on board a brig bound to Boston, and sailed down the river. In about two miles, we passed the nunnery—a pleasant looking building, surrounded by an extensive grove of orange trees. Five miles from the city, we came to the famous battle ground, where Gen. Jackson, and his brave associates " planted a British colony." But this is a matter of history. All the indications of a battle now remaining, are scars of balls on one or two trees.

The large plantations, on both sides of the river, were all alive with negroes, cutting cane and transporting it to the steam mills to make sugar. It appears to me, that slavery sits lighter on the negro race, than it would on any other human beings.— They are, generally, cheerful, and appear to be inclined to make the best of their situation. Much injustice, and many wrongs have been done to the African race. They were torn from their homes, their friends, and their country—carried to a distant land, and sold to hopeless, irremediable slavery. The original kidnappers have much to answer for.

But the case is now somewhat changed. Neither the masters or the slaves, now upon the stage, are the parties to the original transaction. Slavery has existed for a long series of years; and the present owners of slaves obtained possession of them either by descent, or by purchase. They came into their possession, slaves; they did not change their condition. The only fault, therefore, they are justly chargeable with, is the continuance of slavery.— How far culpable the slaveholder may be in this particular, I shall not undertake to decide, any more than I would the degree of guilt justly chargeable to a Mussulman, for believing Mahomet to be a true prophet.

In all the publications and lectures which I have seen and heard upon slavery, it appears to me that

in regard to the present owners of slaves, the subject is not viewed in its true light. Slavery is stated
to be a great evil; and therefore, slaveholders are
great criminals. However well this may sound in
logic, it does not sound well in morals. But there
is another inference drawn from the premises—that
it is the duty of the inhabitants in the non-slave-
holding States, to get up a crusade against the slaveholders. Not with swords and guns to be sure; but
to give them a bad name, render them odious in the
estimation of mankind, and to continue a general
warfare upon their characters. This is, indeed, the
worst kind of warfare. Better take property or life;
for what of value has a man left, when deprived of
his " good name?" To this, I shall be answered,
that it is proper to call things by their right names—
a spade ought to be called a spade; and a criminal
ought to be called a criminal. So far as it applies
to slavery, I have two plain replies to make. In the
first place, it is assuming too much to call a slaveholder a criminal, under the peculiar circumstances
of the case; and secondly, if the fact were so, it is
not always good policy to bring accusations against
an individual, if the object be to reform him.

It is a good maxim in law, and in religion too,
that even the truth is only to be spoken from a good
motive and a justifiable end. For the peace and
well-being of society, facts are not to be stated,
merely to outrage the feelings of another, and to
gratify the spleen of the speaker. Now, I would
17

respectfully ask, what good can come of picking up
all the tales concerning cruelty to slaves, whether
true or false, and proclaiming them in the most imposing form upon the house top, to a non-slavehold-
ing audience? Every new case of cruelty is seized
upon with avidity, and exultingly paraded before the
public. This looks a little too pharisaical. 'Lord
I thank thee that I am not as other men are; nor
like unto these wicked slaveholders,' seems to beam
from some men's countenances.

Is it not in accordance with the christian religion,
if a brother offend, to go *privately to him*, and tell
him his fault? Now, if the object be to emancipate
the slaves, *go to the slaveholder himself*, and en-
deavor to satisfy *him* that slavery in itself is evil;
and, on a view of the whole ground, it is safe, practicable, and beneficial to the slaves to be set free.—
To the objection that it would be unsafe to go
among slaveholders for such a purpose, I reply, that
missionaries are sent among the Indians of the West,
the heathen of the East, and in the islands of the
sea; and can it be deemed more dangerous to go
among the slaveholding citizens of the United States,
than among them? It cannot be pretended. The
fact is, a man may travel through the slaveholding
States with perfect safety, provided he carry the deportment of a gentleman, and discuss the subject of
slavery, as all subjects ought to be, in a decent and
respectful manner.

Of this, I cannot doubt, from my own experience in the matter. During a residence of three years in a slaveholding State, and in my various excursions among the planters, I uniformly found hospitable and kind treatment; and a readiness to discuss the subject of slavery with the same freedom that they would any other.

It would be a very good plan for our lecturers on slavery, to travel through the southern States, and see for themselves the true condition of the master and slave. Their censures of their southern brethren might be softened down a little; and they would sometimes feel more inclined to pity than upbraid. They would find the emancipation of slaves not new, or unthought of, by the people of the South; that it is a subject, which has engaged their anxious thoughts, and caused much private and public discussion. The southerners are more willing to emancipate their slaves, than our northern people generally suppose; but the great question is, how can it with safety be done? Some of our northern people would decide this off hand. Only say, " be free," and it is done. But the slaveholder believes, there are many things to be taken into consideration—self-preservation, good order of society, and the condition of the emancipated slave, are all to be regarded and weighed, before freedom is granted.

But I believe the slaveholders do injustice to the character of the negroes in one particular. If they were all emancipated to-day, I do think, there would not be attempts made to murder the whites, as has been supposed. They are naturally a friendly, confiding race—neither ungrateful, or insensible to kind treatment. When they have a good master, and there are many such, they become very much attached to him; and would, unhesitatingly, risk their lives in his defence.

I have been in the fields, where hundreds of slaves were at work, and conversed with them. They appeared to be well clothed and fed, and had an easy task. I thought them to be as lively, gay and happy as any set of beings on earth.

They are very fond of music, and display a good deal of ingenuity, in adapting songs to their various kinds of work and recreations. Many a night, I have raised my window, sat down and listened for hours, to the melody of their voices, in singing their harvest songs, around a pile of corn.

But the danger lies, in turning loose upon the world, a race of beings, without houses, lands, or any kind of property; who are ignorant, gay and thoughtless, and entirely unused to provide for themselves. How preposterous the idea! What rational man would think of it? They must beg, steal, plunder, or starve. If slaves be emancipated, it must be the work of time; and provision must be made, temporarily at least, for their support.

But it is urged, that holding in bondage a human being, is wrong, and therefore, he ought to be set at liberty *immediately*. A person cannot do right, or repent of evil, too soon. As this applies to the slave, it may be false reasoning from just premises. Although it might be wrong for the eagle to catch the mole and bear him aloft into the air, yet would it be right, then to let him go, when he knew the fall would dash him to pieces? The setting at liberty in such a case, would only be inevitable destruction. It would therefore be right, and not *wrong*, to retain possession, until liberty can be granted in safety.

That many individuals are justly chargeable with cruelty to their slaves, there can be no doubt.— Their condition is better in the old, than in the new States. But it appeared to me, that many of the acts of cruelty were negligently suffered by the master to be done, rather than inflicted by him. They are too apt to entrust their servants in the hands of ignorant overseers, who punish without judgment or mercy.

A planter informed me, he was riding along by his field one day, and observing the overseer was preparing to flog a negro, he rode up to inquire into the cause of the punishment. He was informed the negro would not work, alleging he was sick.— He asked the overseer if he had ascertained that the negro was *not* sick. He replied no; for he presumed it was only a pretence to get rid of work. He went up to the negro, examined his pulse and tongue, and found he had a high fever. He told the negro to take a horse from the plough, and ride home, and he would come directly and see he was

17*

properly attended to. He then turned to the overseer, and told him he was not a suitable man to have the care of human beings—and discharged him on the spot.

In Texas, I saw a negro chained in a baggage wagon, for the purpose of carrying him home to his master. He told me he ran away from him, three months previous, and had all that time lived in the woods, and obtained his food by hunting. He said his master was a cruel man, flogged him unmercifully, made him work hard, and did not feed or clothe him well. At night, an axe *happened* to be left in the wagon, and he liberated himself and escaped. On enquiry, I found the negro's story to be true.— The master was all he had represented him to be, and his conduct was generally reprobated by the people. As I was walking on the seashore, I again came across the negro. He recognized me at once ; came to me, and begged that I would take him with me ; and said he would willingly labor for me all the days of his life ; but he could not return to his master. This I could not do ; but was obliged to leave the negro to his fate.

There are many hardships and cruelties incidental to a state of slavery ; but the cruel master is as much despised and reprobated in his own immediate neighborhood, as elsewhere. It is now unpopular every where, to ill-treat the slave. His condition has generally improved ; and the yoke is often made to sit so light, that it is neither felt, or thought of.

But still, slavery in its mildest form is attended with many moral, as well as physical evils ; is wrong in principle, and contrary to the spirit of our free institutions ; and I earnestly hope, that this dark spot on Freedom's bright banner may soon be blotted out forever.

But to effect such a great object as this, will require the wisdom and aid of the North and the South combined. Let " the North give up, and the South keep not back ;" let them amicably take counsel together ; and devise some plan in which the rights, interests and feelings of all parties are nicely balanced and duly regarded.

But I see no way in which slavery can be abolished without the aid of the slaveholders. This kind of property is guarantied to them by the supreme law of the land, and to give it up, must be a voluntary act. It appears to me the course things are now taking at the North, instead of winning the aid of the South, tends directly to brace them against emancipation. It appears to the South as an officious interference in their affairs, in the most offensive form.

What would we think, if the South should employ a scavenger, to pick up all the private and public acts of cruelty of the northern people ; such as the whipping of the boy by Arnold, the starving to death of another, by Fernald, &c. &c. &c. ; and then, set up a press, expressly to blazon forth these cruelties ; and hire itinerant lecturers to go about

and proclaim to a southern audience, in the highest
strains of impassioned eloquence, the wickedness,
corruption and enormities of the citizens of the
North! And say, they " had waited forty years"
for the northern people to reform themselves;
which was time enough, and they would wait no
longer. They, therefore, were justified in holding them up to the scorn and reproach of all human kind! When the North knew, and all the
world knew, they were no better than they should
be at home; that they had work of reform enough
near at hand; and that they had no legal right to
interfere, and could have no legal action upon the
subject. And although the avowed object was the
reform of the northern people, yet they kept aloof
from them, and hurled their poisoned arrows at a
distance, alleging that they might in their patriotic
zeal, so much arouse their indignation, that it would
be unsafe to go near them. What would northern
people say to all this! Should we say, go on, brethren! God speed! Or should we say, this is mean,
cowardly business—empty boasting—gasconade!—
These people may not, indeed, be guilty of this particular thing of which they accuse us; and that is
the very reason why they choose this subject for ac-
cusation—why they walk so proudly erect—ring all
the changes and make the most of it. It is to tri-
umph over us, and build up themselves on our ruins.
There is in truth, a worse kind than negro slavery—

when a man becomes a slave to his own unhallow-
ed, vindictive passions.

Much injustice has been done the southern people. Those who have travelled and dwelt among
them, bear testimony to their highmindedness, kindness and hospitality. They scorn to do an act of
meanness; or to enter upon the broad field of scan-
dal. And although their strong sensibility may
sometimes lead them into error, yet in all the virtues
which ennoble man, they might not suffer in a comparison with the North. If we choose to bring railing accusations against them; they may not descend
to recriminate; but leave us the undisputed occu-
pants of the ground we have chosen. And we may
have the sore mortification at last to find, we have uttered anathemas in vain; and brought nothing to
any desirable result—that we have toiled hard, and
effected nothing, but our own humiliation and dis-
grace.

But I must leave the subject of negro slavery.—
Perhaps I have dwelt too long upon it already to
comport with the design of this book. It is a great
and an important subject; and to do it justice,
would require a volume. It is my solemn conviction,
however, that for the northern people to effect any
thing, towards the freedom of the African race,
much prudence must be exercised, and conciliatory
measures adopted; so as to enlist the undivided en-
ergies of the South in the great work of emancipation.

We were three days sailing down the river. Just at night the pilot came aboard, took us over the bar at the southwest pass, and we put out to sea, with a strong, fair wind from the northwest. The muddy waters of the Mississippi are seen far out to sea, even after you lose sight of the land. There was another passenger besides myself; and the violent rolling of the vessel soon made us dreadfully seasick. This, with me, lasted but three days; but the other passenger was sick during the whole voyage, and suffered incalculable pain and distress.

There are many things disagreeable to a landsman in a voyage at sea. And in the first place, the rolling of the vessel. This is always disagreeable, but often it is so vehement that you cannot stand, walk, or sit without much caution and trouble. While food is eaten, you must hold on to the plate with one hand, and wield the knife with the other, and this is often done at the imminent hazard of "marring the corners" of the mouth. Sometimes, in spite of all exertion, a sudden lurch will throw you off the balance, and you get a bowl of hot coffee in your lap. And then, at night, you are tossed to and fro in the berth, so that you cannot soundly sleep, and arise in the morning more fatigued than when you laid down.

And this motion of the vessel produces seasickness—an affliction exceedingly grievous to be borne. I had been seasick ten or a dozen times in my life, and this was the third time on my present tour;

and I tried all the precautionary means I had ever heard of, but without any beneficial effect. Could any effectual remedy be discovered, it would save a vast amount of human distress.

The shoreless ocean, seen day after day, affords but a dull and barren prospect to a landsman. The only variety seems to be, when a storm arises; and then, it puts on such a terrific form, that the sublimity of the scene cannot be fully enjoyed. We had a severe blow off the coast of Florida ; but the shivering of sails, and the mountains of foam dashing over our frail bark, caused fear to predominate over every other sensation.

The complete and rapid change of the scene at sea, is sometimes very striking. We would be quietly sailing along with a gentle breeze, just enough to fill the sails, and keep the vessel in motion on her course ; when all at once, a violent squall arises, suddenly strikes the ship, whizzes through the rigging, fills the sails to bursting, and drives her rapidly on, through billows of foam. The captain stands upon the quarter-deck, gives his orders through the speaking trumpet—the sailors run aloft, cling to the yards and take in sail. The contrast is indeed great. One moment, all is calm and quiet; the next, all is uproar and confusion ; and could one feel entirely at ease, it would be a great source of amusement, during a long voyage.

But a sailor's life is one of care, hardship, watchfulness and anxiety. Our captain would walk the

deck for hours, anxiously watching the whole circle
of the horizon—the appearance of the clouds and
the direction of the wind. Of a sudden, he would
stop short, call all hands, order the light sails taken
in, and close-reefed those that remained ; when to
my unpractised eye, there was no cause of alarm, or
appearance of a change of weather. But the result
would invariably show the correctness of his opinion. In no one instance, did he prematurely take in
sail, nor did the squall ever come and " catch him
napping."

The third day out, from the mouth of the river,
we saw the highlands of Cuba. On the fifth, the
Sand Key lighthouse, on the Florida shore. We
saw no other land on the voyage, except a small isl-
and on the Little Bahama Banks, until we came in
full view of the village of Chatham, fifty miles south
of Boston. The wind became fair, the weather thick
and rainy. The next day, twenty miles out, the
pilot came aboard, and we run safely into Boston
harbor. We had been just twenty-five days from
New Orleans—a distance of twenty-five hundred
miles. We had experienced all the varieties of a
sea voyage—light winds, calms, strong breezes and
storms—and now, with no small degree of pleasure,
I again set my foot on *terra firma.*

The following day, I took the stage and arrived
home at Exeter; having been absent about five
months, and having travelled by land and water the
distance of eight thousand miles. I passed over

the whole route without arms, and at no time did I feel the need of any. I was uniformly well treated ; and often received kind attentions, and found many acquaintances whom I left with regret, and shall remember with gratitude.

The weather had, generally, been mild and pleasant. The greatest indication of cold weather I found on the whole trip was a slight frost. On returning at once to the region of severe cold weather, I found it exceedingly oppressive. Our northern winters are indeed long, severe and crabbed ; and were the people as crabbed as the climate, life would become altogether intolerable. But the southern and western climate is far more bland and mild, and much more grateful to the feelings than ours ; and this, together with the facility of obtaining all the necessaries and conveniences of life, induces me to believe that a much greater amount of comfort and happiness may there be enjoyed.

And now it only remains, most respectfully to take leave of my readers. Those who have traced the TRIP TO THE WEST AND TEXAS through the foregoing pages, I hope, may have enjoyed all its pleasures, without incurring its attendant hardships and fatigue.

18

APPENDIX.

Some further information of the new country through which I passed, I subjoin in the form of an appendix. In this, I have liberally availed myself of the writings of others, and of such information as could be obtained from travellers. I shall begin with the

Territory of Michigan.

This Territory is bounded by the national boundary line on the east and north, by the Mississippi river on the west, and by the States of Illinois, Indiana and Ohio on the south. These boundaries include a vast extent of territory; but as that portion of it which lies to the north and west of Lake Michigan and the State of Illinois is for the most part a wilderness, having only some small settlements on Green Bay, the Milwake and Mississippi, my remarks will be confined to that part of it commonly called the peninsula, lying between lakes Erie and Michigan.

Population.—This Territory is estimated by good judges to contain between thirty-five and forty thousand inhabitants. The rapid and increasing tide of emigration into it, induces the belief that it will soon be admitted as a State into the Union. Its present and increasing importance may be in a great measure attributed to the enterprising, active and energetic talents of its late governor, Lewis Cass, the present Secretary of War. His personal exertions and enlightened policy, not only facilitated its settlement, but developed its vast and various resources. A large portion of its inhabitants are from New-York and the Eastern States, and are as active and industrious as those are in the sections of country from which they came. They make rapid improvements; and in a few years, the country will not be behind the flourishing State of Ohio, in farms and villages.

Face of the Country.—That part immediately bordering on lakes Erie, St. Clair and Huron, and their connecting waters, is generally rather level and heavily timbered, but somewhat deficient in good water. In the interior, it becomes gently undulating, occasionally well timbered, and interspersed with oak openings, plains and prairies. The plains are frequently covered with such a regular, beautiful and thrifty growth of timber, so free from underbrush, as to wear the aspect of a cultivated forest. They are more easily improved than the heavy timbered land, and produce full as well. The openings are often rather deficient in timber, though they are not unfrequently skirted with plains, or contain patches of woodland, from which an ample supply may be obtained, not only for fuel, but for building, fencing, and all other farming purposes, if used with economy. They usually require but little, and sometimes no labor to prepare them for the plough; three or four yoke of cattle are found to be amply sufficient to break them up the first time, after which they are cultivated with nearly as much ease as old improved lands. They are found to be excellent for wheat, to improve by cultivation, and usually to produce a good crop of corn the first season.

The prairies generally support a heavy growth of grass—are free from timber, and may be divided into two classes. One is called dry, and the other is denominated wet prairies. The former possess a rich soil, are easily cultivated, and generally yield in rich abundance almost every kind of produce which might be expected to flourish in forty-two degrees north latitude, especially those on St. Joseph's river. And the latter often prove serviceable, not only in affording early pasture, but in supplying the emigrant with the means of wintering his cattle; and may, with a little labor, frequently be made to yield an abundant supply of excellent hay. The interior of the territory is well watered with rivers, creeks and small lakes; many of which contain an unusual quantity of fish. There are several salt springs,

18*

which have not yet been tried nor improved, situated in different parts of the territory, all of which have been reserved by the United States ; but it is not certain that any of them will prove very valuable. By boring a number of feet, the water would improve, and might, in some cases at least, not only justify the erection of extensive works for the manufacture of salt, but prove also a source of revenue to the United States, as well as afford to the manufacturer the means of accumulating wealth.

The surveyed part of the territory is laid out by the United States into townships of six miles square, which are divided into thirty-six sections or square miles, containing each six hundred and forty acres. These are subdivided, by imaginary lines, into quarter and half quarter sections; the latter of which contain each eighty acres, is the smallest quantity sold by the United States, and may, as well as the larger tracts, be selected by the purchaser. Though there is a small tract of land which proves rather unhealthy at the mouth of Huron, Saginaw and Rouge rivers, as well as at the mouth of Brownstown and Swan creeks, owing to the sluggishness of the water at the outlet of these streams, yet the climate of the surveyed part of the territory is mild, lying between forty-one degrees thirty-nine minutes, and forty-two degrees thirty-four minutes north latitude. The air is salubrious, and the water generally clear. The soil, which produces in rich abundance wheat, rye, barley, oats, peas, beans, Indian corn, and potatoes, as well as all kinds of vegetables usually cultivated in the same latitude, consists of such a variety, that it cannot fail to suit the choice of almost every person in the pursuit of agriculture.— Fruit, of course, has not yet been tested in the interior, for the want of time, except peaches, which do exceedingly well; but if I may be permitted to draw an inference, from the quality of the various kinds which grow in great abundance on the French plantations, along the margin of Detroit river, as well as on other parts of the great chain of navigable waters, then I presume I shall be allowed to say, that the soil of Michigan is equal, for the production of fruit to that of any State in the Union. The pear trees along this river, which were planted in the early settlement by the French, are remarkably large, very tall, and extremely thrifty and beautiful, and bear a most delicious fruit, which generally sells from two to four shillings per bushel. Apples, at Detroit, vary from twelve to fifty cents, and may generally be procured by the bushel, for the latter price, even in winter. Cider, in the fall, is from one and a half to two dollars per barrel, for the juice. Currants, blackberries, black and red raspberries and cherries bring from three to four cents per quart; though the earliest of these, as well as whortle berries and strawberries, command six pence. Plumbs are scarce, because they have not been generally cultivated, though they are likewise found to do well.

The price of unsold wild land is fixed and uniform, being one dollar and twenty-five cents per acre, the terms ready money, and the title indisputable, as it comes direct from the United States, under the seal of the President. The richest, most fertile, and perhaps more beautiful part of the territory, is generally thought to be adjacent to the St. Joseph's river and its various branches; which, from present appearances, bids fair to become speedily settled; settlements began to form on it a year before it was offered for sale. It only came in market in May, 1834, and such has been the influx of emigration to this part of the territory, that the Legislature in October last, formed twelve new counties, mostly thereon, and organized two of that number. This part of the territory possesses several copious mill streams, particularly Hog-creek, the Dowagiake, Christianna, Pigeon, Crooked and Portage rivers, a few of which have already been improved, by the erection of saw and grist mills. The climate of this part of the territory, though mild, is apparently more subject to wind than the valley of the Ohio river. The prevailing wind is the southwest; and as it crosses a large tract of prairie country in Illinois and Indiana, comes here with much force, and in winter is somewhat piercing. Considerable snow falls; nevertheless it is very favorable to wheat, rye, potatoes and turnips, and though not very adverse, yet not so congenial as the valley of the Ohio river, to southern corn and the more tender grains and esculents.

Fruits, of course, have not yet been cultivated here, except a few apples and peaches, by the French, which appear to do well.

The prairies in this quarter are of the richest soil, and may be ploughed in two days after the frost leaves the ground in the spring. They usually produce thirty or forty bushels of wheat to the acre; and from thirty to eighty of corn have been raised from the same quantity of ground, in all the prairies that have as yet been occupied : four hundred acres of corn were cultivated on Beardsley's prairie last year, which having been improved the year before averaged fifty bushels to the acre. These prairies not unfrequently produce thirty or forty bushels of corn to the acre, the first season, without being ploughed or hoed after planting.

The surveyed part of the territory is divided into three United States land districts, containing each one land office; one of which is at Detroit, one at Monroe and one at Bronson, in the county of Kalamazoo.

The rivers Grand, St. Joseph, Raisin, Huron, Clinton, Rouge, Kalamazoo and Shiawassee, interlocking in different parts of the territory, not only irrigate the country in a beautiful manner, but offer unparalleled inducements for canaling, and with comparatively but little expense, as there would be no mountains, nor probably rock strata to cut through. It is already in contemplation, by means of the Grand river and Clinton, or the St. Joseph's

and Raisin, to open a water communication across
the peninsula, by means of a canal, which would
terminate at Detroit or Monroe ; and probably at no
distant period, it will not only be undertaken, but
will be accomplished in such a manner as to accommodate both these places in this respect. A company was incorporated, by an act of the Legislature,
last fall, under the title of the " Summit Portage
Canal and Road Company," with a capital of ten
thousand dollars, to be divided into one thousand
shares of ten dollars each, for the purpose of cutting a canal west of Lake Michigan, to connect the
Fox and Ouisconsin rivers at what is usually termed
the Portage of the Ouisconsin, and to construct a
turnpike road on said portage, parallel to said canal;
and also to construct another turnpike road from the
lower extremity of the rapids of the Kaukauin, on
the east side of the Fox river, on the most direct
and eligible route to Winnebago lake, and for the
erection of piers, wharves, warehouses and other
public buildings and improvements, in and about
said canal and turnpike, for commercial purposes.—
Michigan extends at present west to the Mississippi
river ; but it is expected the territory will shortly be
divided, and a new territory set off west of Lake
Michigan ; and organized by the name of Ouisconsin or Huron. The territory was originally owned
and occupied by emigrants from France ; consequently the old inhabitants or first settlers are mostly French.

WAYNE COUNTY—contains about seven thousand inhabitants, many of whom are French. Its seat of justice is Detroit. Hamtranck, Detroit and Springwells. These towns, which lie in the northeast part of the county, border on Detroit river, and are rather level, and but poorly supplied with water. The northern part of the two latter is somewhat broken by marsh and wet prairie; but near the centre of Springwells is a tract, containing some excellent arable land not yet entered, lying within from six to ten miles of Detroit, where a new settlement has recently been formed, and through which a road has lately been opened, leading from Detroit to Farmington. The towns of Pekin, Nankin and Plymouth are well supplied with water by the river Rouge and its various branches, which afford several eligible mill sites, and which have already been advantageously improved by the erection thereon of saw and grist mills. Pekin is heavily timbered with white and black ash, white and black oak, beech, maple and sugar tree. The land is rolling, and the soil rich and fertile, consisting of sand, loam and some clay. The northern and southern part of the town of Nankin has much the same appearance as Pekin, though the soil is more sandy, and requires less labor to cultivate it; yet it yields quite as well; but the middle is plains and openings, of an inferior quality and soil. Plymouth has likewise a similar appearance to Pekin, though the northern part is more rolling, yet even here the timber is the same,

with the addition of black walnut; but the soil is
generally of a superior quality.

Huron.—This town is watered by a delightsome
river, of the same name, whose waters are very
transparent and abound with fish. It runs through
the town diagonally, exhibiting in many places rich
bottom lands, often bounded on one or both sides by
high sloping banks, and not unfrequently skirted
with beautiful plains. Though a great proportion
of this town is rather destitute of running streams,
yet the soil in general is fertile, and for the most
part easily cultivated. The eastern part is oak
openings and plains of a good quality, interspersed
with groves of heavy timber which often contain a
small black ash swamp, and sometimes a wet or dry
prairie; but the south part is heavily timbered with
white and black ash, white oak, beech and maple,
with occasionally a whitewood. The southwest
corner is low land, and contains a large wet prairie.

Brownstown is watered by the Huron river, Muddy and Brownstown creeks. The northwestern part
of this town is but poorly watered, and exhibits alternately oak openings, plains and prairies, occasionally interspersed with groves of heavy timber. The
southeastern part is rather level and heavily timbered, except small tracts at the mouths of Huron river
and Brownstown creek, which consist of prairies
that are more or less inundated with water.

Montguagon embraces Gross' Isle, and is situate
on Detroit river. It is gently undulating, possesses

a fine quarry of limestone, and a rich soil, supporting a thrifty and heavy growth of white oak, hickory, beech, maple, white and black ash.

MONROE COUNTY—contains a population of about
four thousand, many of whom are French. There
are three villages in this county, namely, Monroe,
Frenchtown and Port Lawrence. The first of these,
which is the seat of justice for the county, is a flourishing village situate on the river Raisin, about six
miles from Lake Erie, and thirty-six from Detroit.
The United States turnpike, from the latter place to
the Ohio State line, passes through it, and here was
situated the bank of Monroe. It possesses an ample supply of water power for propelling hydraulic
machinery, a part of which has already been converted to the use of saw and grist mills, as well as
to the use of machines for carding and dressing
cloth.

The United States have made a survey of Plai-
sance Bay harbor, at the mouth of the river, with a
view of improving the same. Monroe is now the
second village in the peninsula, as it regards population; and should they succeed in forming a good
harbor at the mouth of the river, as it possesses
water power, it may yet equal, if not rival Detroit.
The county is generally well watered; the northeastern part is rather level and heavily timbered;
but the western and southern part is rolling land,
alternately abounding in prairies, openings, or heavy

19

groves of timber. The soil of this county is uniformly rich, and of a very superior quality.

WASHTENAW COUNTY—contains about four thousand inhabitants, who are, with a few exceptions, Americans. Its seat of justice is Ann Arbor, a village of five years growth, situate on the river Huron, forty miles west of Detroit, containing about ninety dwelling houses. Ypsilanti, the second village in the county as to population, is likewise situate on the Huron, about ten miles below Ann Arbor, at the place where the United States turnpike, from Detroit to Chicago, crosses it.

This county contains twelve mercantile establishments, three distilleries, one fanning mill factory, one oil factory, one gunsmith, one wagon maker, five flouring mills, thirteen saw mills, and two machines for carding and dressing cloth. It abounds in select and common schools, and contains many mechanics. Its surface is gently undulating and beautiful; and its soil prolific, consisting of a deep black sand, loam and some clay. It exhibits in succession, beautiful prairies, oak openings, and heavy groves of timber, consisting of white, red and black oak, beech, walnut, whitewood, bass, elm, maple and butternut, with almost all other kinds that usually grow in forty-two degrees of north latitude, evergreen excepted. The river Huron, of Lake Erie, meanders through the centre of it north and south; is navigable for boats and rafts to the lake, and with its several branches waters the middle;

the head waters of the Shiawassee the north, and
the rivers Raisin and Saline and their branches, the
south part of said county. It has numerous and
extensive water privileges for facilitating manufac-
tures.

MACOMB COUNTY—contains about two thousand
five hundred inhabitants, a considerable number of
whom are French. The northeastern and eastern
part of this county is in general rather level, and
for the most part heavily timbered ; yet it is sufficiently uneven to drain off and leave no stagnant
waters ; but the western part is rolling land, somewhat broken, being very hilly and uneven, and consisting of oak openings, plains, and some prairie
land.

The plains are remarkably free from underbrush,
and are, as well as the prairies and openings, very
rich and fertile, producing not only wheat, but every
other kind of grain in rich abundance. The Clinton river, together with its numerous tributaries, irrigate this county in a beautiful manner. It possesses
advantages over many of the peninsular counties,
on account of its proximity to the great chain of
navigable waters. It fronts on lake St. Clair, and
the river Clinton, which runs through the entire
county, nearly in the centre, may easily be rendered
navigable for batteaux, as high up as Rochester.—
And for the accomplishment of which a company
has already been formed, and were incorporated last
fall, by an act of the Legislature. This river is now

navigable to Mt. Clemens, for vessels of considerable burthen; and when the obstructions at the mouth of the river are removed, for which object an application has been made to Congress for an appropriation, then any vessels or steam boats on the lake may come up to the village, a distance of six miles, by water.

This county is very well supplied with water power, it has now in operation seven saw mills, and two grist mills, and embraces four stores, three distilleries, two asheries, and six blacksmith shops. Its seat of justice is Mt. Clemens, a flourishing village situate on the Clinton river, at the place where the United States road from Detroit to fort Gratiot crosses it. It lies four and a half miles from the lake, by land, and twenty northeastwardly from Detroit.

Washington lies in the northwest corner of the county, and consists principally of oak openings and plains, though it has some prairie land. The openings and plains are extremely free from underbrush, and prove to be excellent for the cultivation of wheat. The south part of the town is rolling land, exhibiting a rich, and for the most part a sandy soil, though it is sometimes composed of sand and loam intermixed; but the north part is what is commonly called broken land, being very hilly and uneven, and not unfrequently exhibits granitic boulders in great plenty.

Shelby and Ray consist principally of gently undulating and heavy timbered land, interspersed occasionally with oak openings. They are well watered and possessa very productive soil.

Harrison is in general rather level, and the north part though somewhat swampy is susceptible of being converted into excellent meadow.

Clinton possesses generally a rich soil, is heavily timbered and embraces a marsh or wet prairie of considerable extent on its eastern border adjacent to the lake shore, the greater part of which, however, if properly ditched, would prove to be good natural meadow. The northern part of the town is gently undulating and well supplied with water, of which the southern part is too deficient, being rather level.

OAKLAND COUNTY—contains about six thousand inhabitants, all Americans. It has three villages, each with a mill on its border, namely, Pontiac, Auburn and Rochester; the first of which is the seat of justice for the county, and is situated twenty-eight miles northwest of Detroit, on the Clinton river, where the United States road from Detroit to Saginaw crosses it. This county presents a great variety of soil, and upon examination will be found to suit the choice of almost every person in the pursuit of agriculture. The rivers Clinton, Rouge and Huron, interlocking in different parts extend their many branches, and irrigate the county in a beautiful manner.

19*

Troy embraces townships one and two south in range eleven east, is situate in the southeast quarter of the county, and is principally timbered land; township two in this town is entirely of this description, is heavily wooded with black and white walnut, linden, white, red and black oak, and the westerly half is of that description usually denominated rolling timbered land, and in quality of soil, is not surpassed by any in the territory; but township one of that description called plains, interspersed with marshes, and is of an inferior quality.

Bloomfield presents a variety of soil, which may be divided into three classes, oak openings, plains and timbered land. The country in the neighborhood of the lakes is oak openings, not so good for grass, but producing wheat in rich abundance—I would mention that two farmers in the vicinity of Wing lake, harvested one hundred and thirty acres of excellent wheat the last season. The north of Bloomfield is of this description, but the south part is timbered land.

Pontiac is generally oak openings of a good quality, but inferior to the lands of Bloomfield.

Oakland.—The south part of this town is timbered land with a rich soil, and the north part plains and openings of a good quality.

The town of Troy is watered by a branch of the Rouge, and the branches of Red river which empty into the Clinton. Bloomfield is watered by three branches of the Rouge, which, meandering through the county, enable every farmer to partake of their privileges. The towns of Pontiac and Oakland are watered by the Clinton river, Paint and Stony creeks and the extreme branches of the Huron. All these streams possess great privileges for hydraulic machinery. The towns of Pontiac and Oakland now contain twelve saw mills, four flouring mills, three fulling mills, three carding machines and one woollen factory. In Bloomfield are four saw mills and one grist mill. In Farmington two saw mills and one grist mill. Perhaps no country of like extent so level possesses more water power.

St. Clair County—possesses great commercial advantages, as it lies on the great chain of navigable waters. It is bounded east by lake Huron and the river St. Clair, which separates it from Canada; south by lake St. Clair and the county of Macomb, west by the counties of Macomb and Lapeer, and north by Sanilac. Black, Pine and Belle rivers, Mill creek and their branches, as well as several smaller streams water this county. The first of these streams is navigable for vessels of considerable burthen, as far up as Mill creek; but Belle and Pine rivers are ascended only a very short distance in batteaux. This county is generally rather level, the eastern and southern part is gently undulating, rich, fertile and most heavily timbered, though there is occasionally some prairie land on the border of lake St. Clair, and along the southern margin of St. Clair river. The northern and western part of this county is comparatively of a light, and for the most part sandy soil, though tolerably productive, and interspersed with swamps and lowland. A great proportion of the timber in this quarter is pine, though it is often intermixed with hard wood and not unfrequently interspersed with groves of tamerack, in some instances with spruce, and often on the shore of lake Huron, with red and white cedar.

There are now in operation in this county, several of the most extensive saw mills in the territory, which are constantly engaged in manufacturing pine boards, planks, &c. and which, together with shingles, constitute at present the principal article of trade in the county. And as lumber may be conveyed from this county by water to any port, not only on the great lakes, but on their connecting waters, therefore the pine timber must ultimately become very valuable. Almost all the pine now used at Detroit for building, comes from this county, as it is the only one in the surveyed part of the territory that is well supplied with this valuable building material. The United States road from Detroit to fort Gratiot runs through the centre of this county, and about twelve miles west of the village of Palmer, which is the seat of justice for the county, and which is situate at the junction of Pine and St. Clair rivers, about twelve miles south of fort Gratiot, and sixty by water northeast of Detroit.

St. Joseph's County—is perhaps the best in the territory, both as to water privileges and the fertility of its soil. It is watered by the St. Joseph's river, and its various branches, many of which afford numerous water privileges, particularly Hog creek, Pigeon, Portage and Crooked rivers, which may be considered copious and excellent mill streams. A saw mill has already been put in operation on Crooked river, and several others have been commenced on the same creek and about Pigeon prairie. The water in this county is uniformly pure and healthy, the climate mild, and the face of the country moderately undulating; consisting principally of oak openings and prairies. There is however a sufficiency of timber in it generally, and from the Grand Traverse on the northwest side of the river St. Joseph's, as high up I believe as Portage river, is a belt of excellent timbered land which is well supplied with water. The principal prairies in this county are Sturges, Nottawa Sapee and White Pigeon. The first of these, Sturges prairie, has a beautiful appearance, and is exuberant in fertility, but is not convenient for water and but tolerably so to good timber—a few families are located on it. Nottawa Sapee, part of which is embraced within the Indian reserve, is an excellent prairie and settlements have commenced on it. But Pigeon prairie is the most valuable one in the St. Joseph's country, as well as the most densely peopled, and perhaps it will not be deemed invidious to say it is the best settlement in the St. Joseph's country, whether we regard the number of its inhabitants or their intelligence and wealth. The soil of these prairies may be considered equal to that of any land in the United States. The usual mode of cultivating these, as well as all other prairies in the vicinity of the river St. Joseph's, is to break up the soil immediately with the plough, at the same time dropping the corn on the edge of the furrow in such a manner that it may be covered by the succeeding one ; in this manner without any other cultivation, they often produce thirty to fifty bushels of corn to the acre the first season, though sometimes it becomes necessary to go through and cut down some of the rankest weeds. The counties of Branch, Barry and Eaton, and all the country north of township four, north; west of the principal meridian, south of the county of Michilimackinac, and east of the line between ranges twelve and thirteen west, and of Lake Michigan is attached to St. Joseph's.

CASS COUNTY—contains a population of two thousand, and is likewise watered by the St. Joseph's river and its branches, several of which afford good mill privileges, particularly the Dowagiake and Christianna, which are rapid and durable streams. A mill has already been erected and is now in operation on the Christianna, near Young's prairie.

The face of this county is similar to that of St. Joseph's county ; though some parts are undulating, yet in general it is level, sufficiently uneven however to drain off and leave no stagnant waters. The timber is principally oak, ash, elm, sugar tree, cherry black and white walnut and hickory, with a variety of other kinds intermixed. The country is generally open, and you can ride with a wheel carriage through the wood land with almost the same ease you can over the prairies, being not in the least interrupted with underbrush. In every part of the county the roads are good. Though some parts of it are but thinly timbered, yet along the Dowagiake from its source to its mouth there is a broad belt of excellent timbered and very rich land, from one to several miles wide, also along the upper portion of the Christianna, extending north of its source, and thence across to the Dowagiake is a fine belt of woodland. This county includes within its boundaries the following prairies, namely, Four Mile, Beardsley, Townsend's, McKenny's, La Grange, Pokagon and Young's, besides several smaller ones, not however known by any particular name. The prairies here are of the richest quality of soil ; may be ploughed in two days after the frost leaves the ground in spring, and frequently produce thirty or forty bushels of corn to the acre the first season, without being ploughed or hoed after planting. The three last mentioned prairies are conveniently situate to mill streams, and principally surrounded with heavy timbered land, but they are nearly all taken up by purchasers. Four Mile prairie is not so happily situate with regard to mills or timbered land ; but nevertheless is fast filling up. From thirty to

eighty bushels of corn and forty of wheat are usually raised from an acre in all the prairies where the
soil has been subdued by previous cultivation.—
Every other kind of grain as well as vegetables are
produced in about the same proportion.

The only town yet laid out in this county is Ed-
wardsburgh, which is the temporary county seat. It
is situate on the border of Pleasant lake, and on the
northeast corner of Beardsley's prairie. The United
States road from Detroit to Chicago passes through
it, as well as the road from fort Wayne to Pokagon,
to Niles', to Young's and to Townsend's prairies,
and to Coquillard in Indiana. All these places except fort Wayne are situate within ten miles of it.
From the town platt, or village, you have a view
not only of the prairie, but also of Pleasant lake.—
The prairie is four miles in extent and the lake
covers about one hundred acres. Fish are abundant
in all the streams and small lakes—forty-three that
would weigh from one to three pounds were caught
with a hook and line in Pleasant lake by two persons in thirty minutes. The water in this lake is
very pure, you can see the bottom where the depth
of water is fifteen feet. The country is healthy,
several large families who settled here before the
land was offered for sale, and who have resided here
for three years, have not had a case of fever nor any
other kind of sickness, except what has resulted
from accident.

The counties of Berrien and Van Buren and all the country north of the same to Lake Michigan is attached at present to Cass county.

BERRIEN COUNTY, not organized, has in it a large proportion of superior timbered land, but has no prairies of much importance. The settlements in this county, though few, are scattered along the river, and the population does not exceed thirty-five families. But, from the nature of the country I am inclined to believe it will be the most populous county on the St. Joseph's.

The rich timbered land, though now avoided for the prairies, will ultimately be in demand, and will afford many dense and excellent settlements.— Through the timbered land in this county run several small creeks, which, with their numerous branches afford an additional convenience to the farmer which he cannot enjoy in the prairies nor in the barrens. Besides the heavy timbered and prairie land, there are large tracts of what are here called barrens, being of a light soil comparatively speaking, though very productive, and which are thinly covered with white and black oak, sometimes of stinted growth, but mostly of a handsome and useful size. The soil is generally a fine sand, mixed with decayed vegetables and sometimes gravelly, with here and there a granitic boulder. The soil of the timbered land is of a loose sandy nature, black with fertility, and eminently adapted to culture. That of the prairies is nearly of the same nature after the sod has been reduced by repeated ploughing. In the timbered land we find white and black walnut, several kinds of ash, also oak, poplar, lynn, beech, elm, hickory, sugar tree, &c. The southeast part of this county is well supplied with water, and possesses several mill sites, some of which have already been improved. Ford's saw and grist mill, on the Dowagiake, have been for some time in operation. There is also a saw mill just ready to commence operation at the mouth of the Dowagiake, and several others have been commenced on the same stream. There is but one village regularly laid out in this county, which is called Niles. It is situate on the St. Joseph's, a short distance above the confluence of the Dowagiake with that river. The first framed house in it was erected in December, 1833. Next summer it is expected there will be considerable building there. Last season, though there were no accommodations, yet by far the greatest portion of merchandize, &c. destined for the St. Joseph's country, when conveyed by water, was landed there.— Next spring will be built two warehouses, there are now two stores and a post office. Post offices have been established at the mouth of the St. Joseph's called Saranac, at Pokagon, southwest corner of town six south in range sixteen west, at Lagrange in the middle of town six south of range fifteen west, at Pigeon prairie, at Sturges' prairie, and at the Grand Traverse.

LAPEER, SHIAWASSEE AND SAGINAW.—These counties are not yet organized, but attached to Oakland county. There are no inhabitants in Lapeer, and but few settlers at present in Saginaw and Shiawassee. The face of these two counties is very similar to Oakland.

SAGINAW—is watered by the Shiawassee, Flint, Cass, Tittibawassee and Hare rivers. The most of these streams are navigable for boats; their junction forms the Saginaw river which is navigable for sloops twenty miles to the village which bears the same name, and which is to be the seat of justice for said county. The United States have established a cantonment here, and laid out a road from this place to Detroit, which is not yet finished. When this is completed, it is more than probable that it will settle as speedily as any county in the territory, as the soil is very favorable to agriculture.

SHIAWASSEE.—The soil of this county is rich, and the face of the country gently undulating, in some instances rolling, exhibiting oak openings and heavy groves of timber. The Shiawassee river which is a beautiful, meandering stream, and navigable for boats and rafts to the lake, with its several branches, waters the middle and southeast part. The head branches of Grand and Looking Glass rivers, the southwest part, and Swartz's creek, the Flint and Mistegayock rivers, the northeast part of said county.

CALHOUN.—This county has lately been organized and its seat of justice is the town of Marshall, pleasantly situated on the north bank of the Kalamazoo river. This river and its branches afford many fine mill privileges. The soil is rich and gently undulating, consisting principally of burr oak openings, which are frequently interspersed with prairies. In the southwest part of the county is a small tract of pine timber.

JACKSON—has lately been organized and its seat of justice is the town of Jackson, situated near Grand river. The west half of it is undulating, and consists principally of burr and white oak openings, interspersed occasionally with prairies. It abounds in springs and possesses a fertile soil. The northeast part is heavily timbered and somewhat intersected with marshes and small lakes. The soil, however, of this part, is rich and well adapted for, meadow. Grand river is an excellent stream of pure water, quick, yet navigable for canoes from its junction with its south branch, quite through the county and to Lake Michigan.

KALAMAZOO.—This is one of the newly organized counties. Its seat of justice is the town of Bronson, pleasantly situated on the south bank of the Kalamazoo river. The land office has lately been removed to this place from St. Joseph. The face of this county in general is moderately undulating, though sometimes rolling. It exhibits principally burr oak openings, interspersed with rich fertile and dry prairies, and not unfrequently intersected with groves of first rate timbered land. The character of the soil is in general either a black sand or a rich loam. In the southeast corner of this county is an excellent tract of woodland, covered with a heavy but beautiful grove of sugar maple. Gull and Round prairies are the two largest in this county, and are equal to any in the territory for beauty and fertility. The first of these, Gull prairie, is situate in the vicinity of a beautiful lake, as well as adjacent to the margin of a romantic creek, both of which bear the same name. This lake is about four miles long, and its waters which are very transparent are said to contain white fish. The creek is very rapid and affords hydraulic privileges equal to any in the territory. Prairie Round, which lies in the southwest part of the county, is about four miles broad, and is principally surrounded with woodland; near its centre there is a beautiful grove of timber of about a mile in diameter, cousisting of sugar maple, black walnut and hickory. This county is well supplied with water. The Kalamazoo river which runs through it is a rapid meandering stream, yet navigable for boats. Its surface is frequently chequered with islands and its banks occasionally broken.

BRANCH.—This county is attached to St. Joseph's. A large proportion of it, particularly the southern part, is heavily timbered land, consisting principally of black and white walnut, sugar maple, whitewood, lynn, and some other kinds in smaller quantities.— The Chicago road which runs through the northern

*20

part of this county, passes principally through oak openings, which are occasionally intersected with prairies.

HILLSDALE.—This county is attached to Lenawee. The north part of it is principally oak openings of a good quality, but the southern part is heavily wooded with sugar maple, whitewood, beach, black walnut, ash, &c. The face of this county is rather uneven and the soil in general consists of a rich black loam. The southern part is timbered land. This county is well supplied with water. The St. Joseph's of Lake Michigan, as well as the St. Joseph's of Maumee, the Grand river, Tiffin's and the river Raisin all head in this county, and with their numerous branches water it in a beautiful manner.

LENAWEE COUNTY—contains at present about fifteen hundred inhabitants. The northern part of this county has much the same appearance as Washtenaw, but the southern part is principally timbered land. It contains a tamerack swamp of considerable extent in the southeast corner, yet notwithstanding, the character of its soil and climate is, generally, very inviting. It is principally watered by the Ottawa creek, Tiffin's and Raisin rivers and their branches. It contains two villages each with a mill on their borders, namely, Tecumseh and Adrian— the former of which is the seat of justice for the county. It is situate at the junction of Landman's creek with the river Raisin, and lies about fifty-five miles southwest of Detroit.

BARRY, EATON AND INGHAM COUNTIES—lie on Grand river and its tributaries. This is the largest river in the peninsula. It empties into Lake Michigan, two hundred and forty-five miles south of Michilimackinac, and forty-five miles north of the mouth of St. Joseph, is sixty rods wide at its mouth, and has sufficient depth of water to admit vessels drawing eight feet. On its south bank, near its entrance into the lake, is a pleasant situation for a town, the land being excellent, and gently inclining to the north and west, giving at the same time a fine view of the river and lake; but the opposite shore at the same place has a sandy, sterile appearance.

For about sixty miles up this river, on the north side, the Ottawas hold possession. There are between eight and nine hundred of these people living along Grand river and its tributaries, but many of their most populous villages are on land now belonging to the United States.

This river is the largest stream that waters the west part of the peninsula of Michigan, being two hundred and seventy miles in length, its windings included, and navigable two hundred and forty miles for batteaux; receiving in its course a great number of tributary streams, among which are Portage, Red Cedar, Looking Glass, Soft Maple, Muscota, Flat, Rouge and Thorn Apple rivers. All of these, except the last named, put in on the right bank of the Grand river. Its south branch rises in the open country, near the sources of the Raisin, and after

pursuing a winding course of thirty miles, meets
with the Portage river, which comes in from the east
and intersects the above branch in town two south
of range one west.

Portage river, which has its course through a chain
of low marshy prairies, is a deep, muddy stream,
about fifteen yards wide at its mouth.   Its branches
interlock with those of the Huron of lake Erie,
and the Indians pass from the former into the latter,
with their canoes, by crossing a portage of one mile
and a half.   It is probable that at no distant period,
a canal will be constructed near the route of these
two rivers, so as to afford a safe and easy inland communication between lakes Erie and Michigan.   The
distance from Detroit to the mouth of Grand river,
by way of Michilimackinac, is five hundred and
sixty miles.   This route in the spring and fall is attended with much uncertainty ; and, in case of a
war with the English, the navigation of the straits
of Detroit and St. Clair would be rendered doubly
dangerous.   These difficulties would be obviated by
a communication by water, through the interior.—
The land at the Portage rises forty or fifty feet above
the level of the streams on each side ; but a level
prairie two or three miles to the west of that place,
is said to extend from one river to the other.

From the junction of the Portage and south
branches, this river pursues a northwest course till
it meets with Soft Maple river, in town seven north,
of range six west ;   receiving in that distance Red

Cedar and Looking Glass rivers from the east, and Grindstone, Red and Sebewa creeks from the south and southwest.

Grindstone creek, so named from a sandstone ledge through which it runs, empties into the river about twenty miles below the mouth of the Portage branch. It is twenty miles long, affording several good sites for mills, and runs mostly through an open beautiful country; but is in some instances skirted with bottoms of heavy timbered land.

From the mouth of this creek to that of Looking Glass river, a distance of forty-five miles in a direct line, the Grand river runs through a tract of timbered land, which is several miles in extent on each side, abounding in creeks and springs of water, and bearing a growth of maple, basswood, cherry, oak, ash, whitewood, elm, black walnut, butternut, and some other kinds in lesser quantities. Below Looking Glass river, for forty or fifty miles, tracts of open land are found along the banks, but extensive forests immediately in the rear. The river bottoms are from a quarter of a mile to one mile in width, and the timber lands are covered with a rank growth of rushes, (Equisetum hyemale) on which the Indians keep their horses during the winter. It is found that cattle and horses do better on these rushes, than when kept on hay; and it would seem from their abundance, that nature here intended them as a substitute for that article. The surface of the land after leaving the river bottoms is rolling; and it rises sufficiently high to give rapidity to the numerous creeks that so abundantly irrigate this part of the country.

Red Cedar river is thirty-five yards wide, and puts in about midway between Grindstone creek and Looking Glass river. It rises in Washtenaw and Shiawassee counties, and can be ascended in small boats twenty-five or thirty miles. A few miles below the mouth of this stream, is a ledge of sandstone, which forms a perpendicular wall of twenty-five or thirty feet in height, on each side of the river. This ledge consists of square blocks of stone, of a suitable size to be used in building, and which are rendered more valuable, from the circumstance of their being on the banks of a large navigable river, which with its tributaries, will facilitate its transportation to various sections of the territory.

A bed of iron ore has been discovered in the northeast bank of the river immediately below this ledge ; and, indeed, many of the stones in the lower part of the ledge, have a great resemblance to blocks of cast iron—presenting a rusty surface, very dense, and when broken, have, in a striking degree, the color and appearance of iron itself.

Four miles above the mouth of the Looking Glass river, is the village of P'Shimnacon, (Apple land,) which is inhabited by eight or ten Ottawa families, who have a number of enclosed fields, in which they raise corn, potatoes, and other vegetables usually cultivated by the Indians. The village receives its name from the Pyrus Coronaria, (Crab Apple,) which grows in great abundance on the rich bottoms in its vicinity. Sebewa creek puts into the river on the southwest side, one mile above this village. It is about twenty miles long, sufficiently large for mills, and for the last four miles is very rapid, with a hard, stony bottom.

Looking Glass river which is about forty yards wide, rises in Shiawassee county, and can be ascended in canoes almost to its source. The country near this river, for fifteen miles above its mouth, is what may be termed first rate timbered land ; but above that point it is of an inferior quality, more open, and abounding in tamerack swamps and wet prairies.

It is about eight miles by land from the mouth of Looking Glass to that of Soft Maple river, which is about sixty yards wide at its entrance into Grand river. It heads in Shiawassee and Saginaw counties, and runs nearly a due west course until it unites with Grand river, at the Indian village of Chigaumish-kene. This village consists of twenty-five houses, and has a population of near two hundred souls under the noted chief Cocoose. Here is about one thousand acres of bottom land, of a deep, black soil, that has been cleared by the Indians ; a part of which they still occupy as planting ground ; but the land at this village, as well as that at P'Shimnacon, has been ceded to the United States, and will no doubt, in a short time, be occupied by an industrious

white population. There is a large trail leading
from this village, by way of Shiawassee to Detroit,
a distance of one hundred and thirty miles.

The Grand river here changes its course; and,
with the exception of twelve miles in length, below
Rouge river, runs nearly a west course to Lake
Michigan.

Two miles further down, is the entrance of Muscota river, (River of the Plains,) which comes in
from the north, with a rapid current, and is about
forty feet wide. The country through which it runs
is but little known, as no lands have been surveyed
north of Grand river, below Soft Maple.

It is eighteen miles by land from the mouth of
Muscota to that of Co-cob-au-gwosh, or Flat river,
with several considerable creeks putting into Grand
river, on each side, in the intermediate distance.—
Ke-wa-goosh-cum's Indian village is situate immediately below the mouth of Flat river, and consists
of sixteen lodges. It is supposed that the line between the United States and the Indian lands will
intersect the Grand river near this place.

Flat river is a shallow stream, about eight rods
wide; and in ascending has a general course of north
by northeast. Of the country along this river, but
little is at present known. It is reported, however,
to be of a hilly, broken aspect; and many places
near its source, to abound in lakes and swamps.—
There is a small lake that discharges its waters into
this river, about sixty miles above its mouth, in

which it is said by the Indians, that white fish are found in great numbers—a circumstance that is rendered more extraordinary, from the fact that this fish has never been seen near the mouth of Grand river, although it is often taken near the entrances of most of the other tributaries of Lake Michigan.

It is ten miles from Flat to Thorn Apple river, which comes in from the south, and, with its numerous tributaries, waters a large extent of country.— Its main branch rises in town two and three north of range three west, and after running a westerly course for more than forty miles, it takes a northward direction, in which it continues until it empties into Grand river, in the south part of town seven north of range two west.

There is a suitable proportion both of open and timber land along this stream, and a great part of each kind may be termed first rate. Two Indian villages are situated at the distance of twenty and twenty-six miles up this river, and another at its mouth, under the Ottawa chief Nong-gee. The last mentioned village is inhabited by twelve or fourteen families who are by far the most industrious and respectable band that reside in that part of the country.

Rouge river, is twenty miles, including the meanderings, northwest of Thorn Apple river. It is about forty miles long, rising near the sources of the Maskegon, and has its banks shaded by lofty forests of white pine. From this place to Muck-a-ta-sha's

21

village, a distance of twelve miles, the Grand river pursues a south direction ; after which it runs nearly a due west course to Lake Michigan.

Six miles above the mouth of the last mentioned inlet, is a rapid of one mile in length, where the river, which is here fifty-two rods wide, is supposed to fall twenty-five feet. The banks at the head of the rapid, are not more than four feet above the level of the river, and they keep a horizontal level until you arrive at the foot of the rapid, where they are nearly thirty feet above the water ; and consequently afford convenient opportunities for profitably appropriating a part of the river, by means of a canal or sluice, to the use of mills or machinery.

There is a missionary establishment, (the Thomas station) at this place, under the superintendence of the Rev. I. M'Coy. The mission family at present consists of a school teacher, a blacksmith, and two or three agriculturists. The school was opened in the winter of 1827, and now has about thirty Indian children, who receive their board, clothing and tuition at the expense of the establishment.

There is a trail leading southwest from the rapids to the Kalamazoo river, and thence to the rivers Raisin and Huron. Another leads directly to the mouth of Thorn Apple river, a distance of only ten miles on the trail, but twenty-five round the curve of the river. The country within this bend, excepting immediately along the river, is of a rough, hilly character, a great part consisting of oak openings, of a barren appearance, with a few scattering groves of white pine. Most of the land, however, in the neighborhood of this tract, is of a good quality, and timbered with all kinds that usually grow on rich alluvial soils.

There is a salt spring four miles below the rapids, which rises out of the ground about half a mile from the river on the east side. The water is said to be, both as to quantity and quality, sufficient to warrant the establishment of works for the manufacturing of that useful article. Near this place is also a bed of gypsum, of a fine quality, which will probably, in time, be of great importance to agriculturists in many of the western parts of Michigan.

Muck-a-ta-sha, or Blackskin's village, is six miles below the rapids, and is near the bend of the river, on an elevated prairie. There is also another village twenty miles lower down the river. From the rapids to the lake, a distance of thirty-six miles, the river is no where less than four feet deep. The current at the former place is too powerful to be ascended with loaded boats. The country along the river for the first fifteen or twenty miles above the lake is generally level, and in many instances swampy, with lofty forests, of various kinds of timber, and bearing an almost impenetrable thicket of undergrowth.

The country watered by the Grand river, consists of between six and seven thousand square miles; and considering its central position in the territory, the general fertility of the soil on the several branches of that stream, the convenience of a safe and good harbor at its mouth, together with its many other important natural advantages, we may be fully justified in the opinion, that it will, at no very distant period, become one of the most important sections of Michigan.

Illinois.

Length, three hundred and fifty miles—breadth, one hundred and eighty. Between thirty-seven degrees, and forty-two degrees thirty minutes north latitude, and ten degrees twenty minutes and fourteen degrees twenty-one minutes west longitude from Washington. It contains fifty thousand square miles, equal to forty millions of acres. It is now divided into fifty-five counties; and by the census of 1830, contains one hundred and fifty-seven thousand five hundred and seventy-five inhabitants; but it probably now contains about two hundred thousand.

Face of the Country.—It is probably as level as any State in the Union. At the northwest of Shaw, neetown, there is a range of hills; and high bluffs are seen along the banks of the Mississippi and Illinois rivers. In the mineral regions at the northwest corner of the State, there are high hills, and the land is somewhat broken; but the largest portion of

the State is composed of gently rolling prairies.—
These prairies are some of them level and wet, but
generally, they are high, dry and gently undulating.
They all have an exceedingly fertile soil, and are
covered with tall coarse grass and a great variety of
beautiful flowers. The soil is a rich, black loam,
entirely inexhaustible, and produces abundant crops
without the aid of manure. In some of the old settled towns at the lower part of the State, the same
spot of ground has been cultivated with Indian corn
for a hundred years, and it now produces equally
as well as it did at first. In the time of strawberries, thousands of acres are reddened with this delicious fruit. But this country, which so delightfully
strikes the eye, and has millions of acres that invite
the plough, wants timber for fuel, building and
fences. It wants good water in many places, and
in too many instances, the inhabitants want health.
These evils will probably all be remedied by the ex-
pedients of cultivation. Bricks will be used for
building; coal and peat will be used for fuel; hedges
and ditches will be made for fences; forests will be
made to grow on the prairies; and deep wells will
be sunk for pure water.

There is a fine tract of rich level land extending
along the eastern shore of the Mississippi about
eighty miles in length, and from three to six miles in
width. It commences near New-Alton, and terminates a little below Kaskaskia. About half of its
width bordering on the river, is covered with a

*21

heavy growth of timber; the remainder is a level prairie; and in the rear it is bordered by a stately bluff of limestone. It is undoubtedly the richest land in the world. Settlements have been made upon it to some extent, but it is not very healthy.— It is called the American Bottom. A bottom very similar to this, either on one side or the other, marks the whole course of the Illinois river.

More than five millions of acres have been surveyed, between the Mississippi and Illinois rivers, and assigned by Congress for military bounty lands. These lands embrace all the varieties of soil found in the State—rich bottoms, swamps, prairies, timbered lands, high bluffs and barrens. The northeast part of it is deemed the most pleasant and healthy.

On Rock river, the Kaskaskia, Wabash, Fox, Du Page, Macoupin and Sangamon are large tracts of first rate land. And very similar to this, are Grand prairie, Mound prairie, the Marine Settlement prairie, and the one occupied by the New-England Christians.

In the region of Sangamon river, nature has delighted to bring together her happiest combinations of landscape; being beautifully variegated with woodland and lawn, like sunshine and shade. It is generally a level country; the prairies are not too extensive, and timber abounds in sufficient quantity to support a dense population. In this beautiful section of the new world, more than two hundred

families, from New-England, New-York and North
Carolina, fixed their habitations before it was surveyed. The land is exceedingly rich and easily cultivated. It now constitutes a number of counties
and is probably as thickly settled as any part of the
State. The Sangamon itself is a fine boatable river,
and has throughout its whole course, pure, transparent water and a sandy bottom. It enters the Illinois river on the easterly side, about one hundred
and forty miles above its mouth.

The Kaskaskia river has a long course in the central part of the State, and the lands upon its borders
are happily diversified with hill, vale, prairie and forest. On its banks are Kaskaskia, the former seat of
government, and Vandalia, the present metropolis.

The region of Rock and Fox rivers is a beautiful
and healthy portion of the State. The land is rich ;
the prairies are high, dry and gently undulating and
surrounded by excellent timber. The only faults
are, the prairies are too large for the quantity of timber, and there are not a sufficient number of springs
and small streams of water. But it is a very pleasant and desirable portion of the country, and I believe more emigrants are now directing their course
thither than to any other portion of the State. It
has one advantage over all the western section of
country, it is more healthy. I believe it is as healthy
as any portion of the United States.

Although there are some bodies of sterile and
broken land in the State, yet as a whole, it contains

a greater proportion of first rate land than any other State in the Union ; and probably as great according to its extent as any country on the face of the globe. One of the inconveniences attending this extensive rich country, is too great a proportion of prairies. They cover more than half of the whole State.— But the prevalence of coal and peat, and the ease with which forest trees may be raised, will render even these extensive prairies habitable.

The original cause of these extensive prairies in all the western and southern country is altogether a matter of conjecture. There is no natural impediment in the soil to the growth of forest trees over the whole extent of the country. It is certain that the fire is the cause of continuing them in existence ; for where the fire is kept out, trees spring up in them in a few years, and their growth is vigorous and rapid.

There are many reasons for the belief, that this western country was once inhabited by a more civilized race of beings, than the present hordes of wild Indians. Specimens of fine pottery and implements of husbandry have been found in various parts of the country; and brick foundations of a large city have lately been discovered in the territory of Arkansas. These, together with the stately mounds and remains of extensive fortifications, indicate that the country was once inhabited by a race of men who cultivated the soil for a subsistence, and were well acquainted with the mechanic arts.

From whence this race of beings came, or whither they went, is alike unknown to us. Since they left, the fire has made the cleared land much more extensive. The fire, in very dry weather and accompanied by a high wind, after scouring over the prairies, takes to the woodland and destroys the timber. Last fall, I saw hundreds of acres of woodland, so severely burnt over, that I had no doubt the trees were generally killed. But in some places, the forest gradually gains upon the prairie; and could the fire be kept within proper bounds, the western country would soon have an abundant supply of timber. But this cannot well be done. The Indian sets the prairie afire, for the conveniency of hunting—the emigrant sets it afire, so that the fresh grass may spring up for his cattle ; and so between them both, they all get burnt over. And when once kindled, the fire goes where the wind happens to drive.

Rivers.—This State has great advantages for inland navigation by means of its rivers. On the east, it is washed by the Michigan lake and Wabash river; on the south, by the Ohio, and on the west, by the Mississippi. The most important river within the State is the Illinois. It rises near the south end of Lake Michigan, runs in a southerly direction about three hundred miles, and falls into the Mississippi, thirty miles above St. Louis. Its two chief head branches are the Kankakee and Oplane ; this latter river runs within twelve miles of the lake, and the space between is a low, wet prairie, so that it might easily be connected with its waters. From the north, comes in the Du Page, a larger stream than the Oplane. At Ottawa, eighty miles south of Chicago, comes in Fox river. This is by far the largest tributary of the Illinois, and at their junction is nearly equal to it in size. In all descriptions of the State, mention is hardly made of Fox river ; but it is the next in size to the Illinois and Rock rivers, and is one of the most beautiful streams in the whole State. It rises in the territory west of Lake Michigan, runs with a lively current, in a very straight channel, from its source to its mouth. It heads in a lake, and this accounts for the fact, that it is not, like other streams, subject to freshets. It is generally fordable—the water is not more than about three feet deep, and the bottom is sand and pebbles. It is a clear stream, abounding in fish, and withal, passes through the most healthy part of the State.

On the west side, nearly opposite Hennipen, comes in the Bureau river. This is a good mill stream, and is composed of two branches, the one called Great and the other Little Bureau ; and these branches join about five miles west of the Illinois. These branches, on the maps, bear the names of Robertson's and James' river, but for what reason I know not. On this river is a large settlement of northern people, and many families from the State of New-Hampshire. Below this, the most material tributaries are the Vermillion and Sangamon from the east, and Spoon river from the west. Whatever others may say, I cannot call the Illinois a pleasant stream. It has a marsh on one side or the other from its mouth to its source, and is full of shoals and sandbars. I passed down the river in a boat that drew less than two feet water, but it often run aground. The worst bar is just below Beardstown. We had to lighten the boat of its freight, water in the boiler, and passengers, before we could pass this bar; and then, the hands had to jump into the water and push the boat over. For about two hundred miles from its mouth, it has many long and narrow lakes, of about the width of the river itself; and probably they were formerly its channel. These lakes generally have an outlet into the river, and these so much resemble it, that a person not well acquainted with the stream, would be puzzled to know what channel to take. The river occupies too much ground for its quantity of water, and for about half of the year, it is a difficult stream to navigate.

Rock river rises beyond the northern limits of the State in the high lands which separate the waters of the Mississippi from those of Lake Michigan. It is a large, beautiful stream, has a lively current, and enters the Mississippi fifty miles below Galena. In the Mississippi near its mouth, is a beautiful island, on which is situated fort Armstrong.

The other principal streams which enter the Mississippi are Fever river, Parasaw, Kaskaskia, and Cahokia. No large streams enter the Ohio or the Wabash, from this State ; but some of them are navigable by keel boats.

Minerals.—In the region of Galena are the richest lead mines in the world. Copper ore has also been discovered. The State abounds in mineral coal, which is excellent for the grate. It burns freer than the Pennsylvania coal, and emits much more light. Salt is made in large quantities at the salt works, near Shawneetown.

Climate.—In the southern part of the State, cotton will grow in a favorable year, and it is cultivated to some extent for family use. This conclusively shows a milder climate than in New-England. In the northern section, in the region of the vast prairies and lakes, the wind sometimes blows strong and keen in the winter. It is not subject to the strong chilly easterly winds so severely felt along the Atlantic coast. During the year, the climate is undoubtedly more mild than that of New-England. Apple, pear and peach trees grow vigorously and produce abundantly. In the spring of the year the air becomes fragrant with the blossoms of fruit trees and wild flowers.

Productions.—The soil and the climate are well suited to the production of wheat, Indian corn, potatoes, and all garden vegetables. The crops are abundant and of an excellent quality. The prairies every where abound in wild grass, and afford an inexhaustible range for cattle, horses and sheep. The grass is very nutricious, and it may with truth be said, there is not a finer grazing country in the world.

Diseases.—The most prevalent diseases are bilious fevers and the fever and ague. These are caused by stagnant water and swamps. Removed from these, good health is generally enjoyed. The consumption, the scourge of New-England, is never known in all the western country. In some parts of the lower section of the State, the inhabitants have been afflicted with a disease called *milk sickness*. It, in the first place, affects the cattle, and never occurs until the frosts of autumn. These frosts kill the grass on the high prairies, and induce the cattle to go into the low bottoms and woods, where vegetation remains green. It has been discovered that the disease is caused by the cattle's eating a poisonous vine which grows luxuriantly in these bottoms. After eating this vine, the animal appears weary and faint, travels with difficulty, droops, and at length dies. If men or animals partake of the milk of the cows, when they are thus disordered, they are affected in the same manner.— Men, however, sometimes recover. This disease is not confined to Illinois. Near the rich bottom lands in Indiana and Missouri, animals and men have been affected with it. In the northern half of the

22

State, I was informed, that not an instance of milk sickness had ever been known.

Chief Towns.—Chicago is now the largest town in the State ; and as it is favorably situated for trade, it will probably continue to take the lead in time to come.   Vandalia is the present seat of government. It is pleasantly situated on a high bank of the Kaskaskia river.   Respectable buildings for the accommodation of the government and the courts have been erected.   The village contains about a hundred houses ; some of them, built of brick and elegant.

Kaskaskia is the oldest town in the State.   It is pleasantly situated on an extensive plain upon the bank of the river of the same name, and eleven miles from its mouth.   It was settled as early as Philadelphia, by the French, and once contained seven thousand inhabitants ; but now it numbers not more than one thousand.   This was formerly the seat of government; it was removed to Edwardsville, then to Vandalia ; but it will probably be destined to take one more remove, either to Springfield or Peoria.

Galena, on the Mississippi, near the northwest corner of the State, began to be settled in 1826.   It is three hundred and fifty miles north of St. Louis, and about one hundred and fifty west of Chicago. It now contains between one and two thousand inhabitants, forty-two stores and warehouses, and two hundred houses.   It is the seat of justice for the

county, and has ten thousand inhabitants in its vicinity. Alton, Jacksonville, Springfield and Peoria
are flourishing villages.

Schools and Seminaries.—The same provisions
here for schools have been made as in the other
western States. In addition to one thirty-sixth part
of all the public lands, three per cent. on all the
sales are added to the school fund. It is in contemplation to establish an university. For this purpose a sixth part of the school fund and two entire
townships have been appropriated. Rock Spring
theological school, under the superintendence of the
Baptists, is a respectable academy in the Turkey
hills' Settlement, seventeen miles east of St. Louis.
It has fifty students. Primary schools are found in
the villages and populous neighborhoods; but in
many places there is much need of them.

Constitution and Laws.—The representatives
and senators are chosen once in two years; the
governor and lieutenant governor in four years.—
The judiciary consists of a supreme court and other county courts. All free white male citizens, who
have resided in the State six months, are entitled to
the right of suffrage; and they vote at elections
viva voce.

Missouri.

This State contains sixty thousand square miles, being two hundred and seventy miles in length and two hundred and twenty in breadth. It lies on the west side of the Mississippi river, between thirty-six and forty degrees north latitude. It now contains, probably, one hundred and fifty thousand inhabitants, of whom thirty thousand are slaves.

Face of the Country, soil, &c.—A large tract of this State, commencing at its south end, extending up the Mississippi river above the mouth of the Ohio, and running into the interior, possesses rich alluvial soil, but is low, swampy, full of lakes, and much of it, subject to overflow. Beyond this to the west, the country is broken and hilly; sometimes covered with a small species of oak, and sometimes naked sandy hills and plains. The whole southerly half of the State, offers but small inducements to the farmer. Where the soil is rich, it is too low and unhealthy; where it is high, dry and healthy, it is too barren and sterile to be cultivated. The best portion of the State lies between the Missouri and Mississippi rivers. This section is the most settled of any part of the State. Its surface is delightfully variegated and rolling, and possesses large tracts of rich alluvial and high prairies. The soil contains a greater proportion of sand, than that of the other western States; so that it is easily cultivated, and is never disagreeably muddy. There are spots where we find the stiff clayey soil of Ohio and New-York; but they are not extensive. No part of the globe, in a state of nature, can so easily be travelled over in carriages as this. Even in spring, the roads cannot be called muddy or difficult to pass. There are two extensive tracts of heavily timbered upland, similar to those of Ohio and Kentucky—the one is called the Bellevue, the other the Boone's Lick Settlement. The surface rolls gently and almost imperceptibly. In this region are many springs of good water, and it is said to be healthy.

The Mississippi is skirted with a prairie, commencing ten miles above the mouth of the Missouri, for the distance of seventy miles. It is about five miles in width, and possesses an excellent soil.

There are no prairies of any considerable size on the borders of the Missouri, within the limits of the State; but its banks are generally covered with a beautiful growth of tall, straight forest trees. The bottom land on this river is about four miles in width, is sufficiently mixed with sand to prevent its being muddy, and is not subject to be overflowed. There are no bayous, ponds or marshes on the margin of the Missouri. The bottoms are now considerably settled for four hundred miles above its mouth. Charaton, over two hundred miles up the river, is the highest compact settlement. But the largest and most populous settlement in the State is Boone's Lick, in Franklin county. This is one hundred and eighty miles above the mouth of the river. Scattered settlements are, however, found along the river banks for six hundred miles, to the Council Bluffs. Above the Platte, which is the largest tributary of the Missouri, the prairies come quite in to the banks of the river, and extend on either hand, farther than can be measured by the eye. This is the general complexion of the river banks until you reach the Rocky mountains.

As far as the limits of this State extend, the river is capable of supporting a dense population for a considerable distance from its banks. Above these limits, it is generally too destitute of wood and water to become habitable by any people, except hunters and shepherds. All the tributaries of the Missouri are generally copies of the parent stream, and one general remark will apply to the whole. They all have narrow margins of excellent bottom land; and as the country recedes from these, it becomes more and more sandy, barren and destitute of water, until it resembles the deserts of Arabia.

Productions.—Wheat and corn are the chief productions, and the soil is excellent for both. The whole western country is remarkable for withstanding the severest droughts. A crop has never been known to fail in the driest seasons. From twenty-five to thirty bushels to the acre is an average crop of wheat, and from fifty to seventy-five, of corn.— The good lands in Missouri produce corn in as great perfection as in any part of the world. It is warm, loamy land, and so mellow that it is easily cultivated.

Even where the sand appears to predominate, great crops are produced. The soil, in the vicinity of the Missouri, is more pliant and less inclined to be muddy, than that on the banks of the Mississippi. Rye, barley, oats, flax, hemp, tobacco, melons, pumpkins, squashes and all garden vegetables flourish remarkably well. Peaches, pears, plums, cherries, &c. grow to great perfection. The land seems well adapted to the use of plaster, and this is found of excellent quality, in inexhaustible quantities, on the banks of the Missouri.

Beyond all countries, this is the land of blossoms. Every prairie is an immense flower garden. In the spring, their prevailing tint is that of the peach blossom—in summer, of a deeper red—then a yellow—and in autumn, a brilliant golden hue.

The natural productions of the soil are abundant. The red and yellow prairie plum, crab apples, paw-paws, persimons, peccans, hazelnu ts and walnuts are generally found in perfection and abundance.— Wild hops cover whole prairies ; and two or three species of grapes are found in various parts of the State. The heats of summer and dryness of the atmosphere render this suitable for the cultivation of the vine. Silk might also be raised in great abundance, as the mulberry tree is every where found among the trees of the forest. Near New-Madrid, cotton is cultivated.

Animals.—Bears, wolves and panthers are found here. The prairie wolf is the most numerous and

mischievous.   Deer, as the Indians retire, grow
more plenty, and are frequently seen in flocks feeding near the herds of cattle.   There is a species of
mole found here, and indeed in all the western and
southern country, called gopher.   These animals
live in communities, and build small eminences of a
circular form and about a foot high.   They are mischievous in potatoe fields and gardens.

Rattlesnakes, copper heads, and ground vipers
are found in the unsettled regions ; especially, near
flint knobs and ledgy hills.   They are not so common as in more timbered regions.   It is probable
that the burning of the prairie destroys great numbers of them.   The waters are covered with ducks,
geese, swans, brants, pelicans, cranes and many other smaller birds.   The prairie hen and turtle dove
are numerous.

The domestic animals are the same as in other
States.   This State and Illinois have decided natural advantages for the rearing of cattle, horses,
hogs and sheep.

Climate, Diseases, &c.—A distinguishing feature
in the climate, is in the dryness and purity of the
atmosphere.   The average number of cloudy days
in a year is not more than fifty, and not more than
half that number are rainy.   The quantity of rain
is not more than eighteen inches.   The sky in summer and autumn is generally cloudless.   There are no
northeast continued rains as in the Atlantic States.
The longest storms are from the southwest.

The usual diseases are intermittent and bilious fevers. Sometimes pleurisy and lung fevers prevail in winter. Pulmonic complaints, attended with cough, are seldom ; and consumption, that scourge of the East, is unknown.

The summers are quite warm, and sometimes oppressive ; but generally, a refreshing breeze prevails. The winters are sometimes cold, and the wind blows sharp and keen. The Missouri is frozen sufficiently strong to bear loaded teams. But days are found even in January, when it is agreeable to sit at an open window. A few inches of snow occasionally fall, but there is hardly any good sleighing.

Minerals.—This State is known to be rich in minerals, although a large portion remains yet unexplored. Lead has been found in abundance.— The principal " diggings" are included in a district fifteen miles by thirty in extent ; the centre of which is sixty miles southwest from St. Louis, and about half that distance from Herculaneum, on the Mississippi. The earth is of a reddish yellow, and the ore is found embedded in rock and hard gravel. Fifty diggings are now occupied, from which three millions of pounds of lead are annually sent to market. It is transported from the mines in wagons, either to Herculaneum or St. Genevieve, and from thence by water to New Orleans. Stone coal abounds, especially in the region of St. Louis and St. Charles. Plaster, pipe clay, manganese, zinc, antimony, red and white chalk, ochres, flint, common salt, nitre, plumbago, porphyry, jasper, porcelain clay, iron, marble and the blue limestone of an excellent qaulity for lime, have already been discovered in this State. Iron, lead, plaster and coal are known to exist in inexhaustible quantities.

Chief Towns.—St. Louis is much the largest town in the State. It is not only the most pleasantly situated, but has the most favorable location for trade of any town on the Mississippi above New Orleans. It has, however, been sufficiently described in the body of this work.

St. Genevieve is situated about a mile west of the Mississippi on the upper extremity of a beautiful prairie. It is principally settled by the French and contains about fifteen hundred inhabitants. It is an old town, and has not increased for the last thirty years.

Jackson, the seat of justice for Cape Girardeau county, is twelve miles west of the Mississippi, contains one hundred houses, some of them built of brick and handsome.

The town of Cape Girardeau is situated on a high bluff of the Mississippi, fifty miles above the mouth of the Ohio. It has a fine harbor for boats, and commands an extensive view of the river above and below. It exhibits marks of decay.

Potosi is the county town of Washington. It is situated in the centre of the mining district, in a pleasant valley sixty-five miles southwest from St. Louis. St. Michael is an old French town among the mines. There are some other small villages in the vicinity of the mining district.

Herculaneum is situated among the high bluffs of the river, thirty miles below St. Louis. There are a number of shot towers in its vicinity. New-Madrid is fifty miles below the mouth of the Ohio. Carondolet is a small French village six miles below St. Louis; and four miles below this, is the garrison, called Jefferson Barracks. The public buildings are extensive, and a large number of soldiers are generally stationed here. There are no large villages on the Mississippi above the mouth of the Missouri. Palmyra is probably as large as any. The others are Louisianaville, Troy and Petersburg.

There are a number of fine villages on the banks of the Missouri; the largest of which is St. Charles, twenty miles from the mouth, and just the same distance from St. Louis by land. It is situated on a high bank of solid limestone, has one street of good brick houses; and in its rear, an extensive elevated prairie. It contains a protestant and a catholic church, was once the seat of government, and numbers [twelve thousand inhabitants; a third of whom are French. It has finely cultivated farms in its neighborhood, and has as interesting scenery as any village in the western country.

Jefferson City is the present seat of government, but being thought to be an unfavorable location has not improved as was expected. It is situated on the south bank of the Missouri, nine miles above the

mouth of the Osage river, and one hundred and fif-
ty-four by water from St. Louis. Fifty miles above
this, is the town of Franklin. It is situated on the
north bank of the river, contains two hundred
houses and one thousand inhabitants. It is surrounded by the largest body of rich land in the State; and
is the centre of fine farms and rich farmers. Boon-
ville is on the opposite bank of the river and was
originally settled by Col. Boone, the patriarch of
Kentucky. Bluffton, two hundred and twenty-nine
miles by water from St. Louis, is the last village
within the limits of this State.

FOREST TREES OF THE MISSISSIPPI VALLEY.

Such forest trees only will be noted, as are not
found in our northern climate. It may be proper
to remark, that the white pine of New-England is
only found in the upper section of the Mississippi
valley—the pitch pine is found in various places on
the high lands, throughout its whole extent; although not on the banks of the streams of water.

The cypress is seen on overflowed and swampy
land from the mouth of the Ohio to the gulf of
Mexico. It is strikingly singular in its appearance.
Under its deep shade, arise a multitude of cone
shaped posts, called 'cypress knees.' They are of
various sizes and heights. The largest generally

seen, are about a foot in diameter at the bottom, two or three inches at the top, and six feet in height. The bark is smooth, and grows over the top end the same as at the sides. The ground, in a cypress swamp, looks as though tapering posts of all imaginable sizes had been set there at random; and are sometimes so thick that it is difficult to ride among them. It has been supposed that these knees are but the commencement of large trees, and there is some reason for this belief; for the tree itself has a buttress that looks exactly like an enlarged cypress knee. A full sized cypress is ten feet in diameter at the ground, but it tapers so rapidly that in ascending eight feet, it is not more than about two feet in diameter; from thence, it rises in a straight smooth column, eighty feet, without any apparent diminution of its size; it then branches off at once in all directions, and forms a level surface of foliage at the top. A forest of cypress looks like a scaffolding of deep green verdure suspended in the air.— The timber is clear of knots, easily wrought, durable, and is the most valuable timber tree in all the southern country.

The live oak is only found near the sea coast. It does not grow tall, but runs out into long lateral branches, looking like an immense spread umbrella. The leaf is small and evergreen. It bears an abundance of acorns, which are small, long and a good deal tapering at each end. Its timber is hard to cut, and will immediately sink in water.

23

The peccan is of beautiful form and appearance, and makes excellent timber for building and rails. It bears a round nut about an inch and a half long and half an inch in diameter. It excels all other nuts in the delicacy of its flavor.

The black locust is an excellent timber tree, and is much used in the building of steamboats. Its blossoms yield an exquisite perfume. The white locust is similar to that of the north.

The black walnut is a splendid tree and grows to a great size. It is much used in finishing houses and in cabinet furniture. It produces a nut very similar to the northern butternut; but the meat is not very palatable. The white walnut is also plenty, as are the various kinds of hickory.

The sycamore is the largest tree of the western forest. One of these trees near Marietta measures fifteen feet in diameter. Judge Tucker of Missouri fitted up a hollow section of a sycamore for an office.

The yellow poplar is a splendid tree and next in size to the sycamore. Its timber is very useful for building and rails. Its blossoms are gaudy bell-shaped cups, and the leaves are of beautiful forms.

The cotton-wood is universally found in all the southern country below the mouth of the Ohio. It is a tree of the poplar class, and somewhat resembles the whitewood of the more northern regions. It is a large stately tree and sometimes measures twelve feet in diameter. One tree has been known to make more than a thousand rails. It derives its name from the circumstance, that when its blossoms fall, it scatters on the ground something much resembling in feeling and appearance short ginned cotton.

The catalpa is found in the region of the cottonwood. It is remarkable for the great size of its deep green leaves, and its rounded tuft of beautiful blossoms of unequalled fragrance. Its seed is contained in a pod about two feet in length, much resembling a bean pod. As an ornamental tree it is unrivalled. In gracefulness of form, grandeur of its foliage, and rich, ambrosial fragrance of its blossom, it is incomparably superior to all the trees of the western world.

The magnolia has been much overrated, both as to the size of the tree and blossom also. It grows up tall and slim; the largest, about two feet in diameter; smooth whitish bark; and slightly resembling the northern beech. Its leaves are of a deep green, small and evergreen. Its blossom is of a pure white, much resembling, although twice the size, of a northern pond lilly. The fragrance is indeed powerful, but rather disagreeable.

There are half a dozen species of laurels; the most beautiful of which, is the laurel almond. It grows to the size of the pear tree; the leaves resemble those of the peach; its blossoms yield a most delicious perfume; and its foliage continues green all the year. It is found in the valley of the Red River.

There is a striking and beautiful tree found on the head waters of the Washita and in the interior of Arkansas, called bow-wood, from the circumstance that the Indians use it for bows. It bears a large fruit of most inviting appearance, much resembling a very large orange. But although beautiful to the eye, it is bitter to the taste. It has large and beautiful leaves, in form and appearance much like those of the orange, but much larger. The wood is yellow like fustic, and it produces a similar dye. It is hard, heavy and durable, and is supposed to be more incorruptible than live oak, mulberry, cypress, or cedar. Above the raft on Red River, the hulk of a steamboat has been built entirely of its timber.

The China tree is not a native of this country, but is much cultivated in the southern regions of the valley for ornament and shade. It has fine long spiked leaves, eight or ten inches in length, set in pairs on each side of a stem two feet long. In the flowering season, the tree is completely covered with blossoms. It bears a small reddish berry, which continues on the tree a long time after the leaves have fallen, and gives it, even then, an interesting appearance. It is a tree of more rapid growth than any known in this country.

The pawpaw is not only the most graceful and pleasing in appearance of all the wild fruit bearing shrubs, but throws into the shade those cultivated by the hand of man. The leaves are long, of a rich green color, and much resemble the leaves of the tobacco plant. The stem is straight, white, and of unrivallèd beauty. The fruit resembles the cucumber, but smoother and more pointed at the ends.— There are from two to five in a cluster; and when ripe are of a rich beautiful yellow. The fruit contains from two to six seeds, double the size of the tamarind. The pulp resembles egg custard. It has precisely the same feeling in the mouth, and unites the taste of eggs, cream, sugar and spice. It is a natural custard; but too rich and highly seasoned to be much relished by most people. So many whimsical and unexpected tastes are compounded in the fruit, that a person of the most sober face, when he first tastes of it, unconsciously relaxes into a smile.

The persimon is found in Missouri, and in the region to the south of it. Its leaves resemble those of the wild cherry, and it grows about the size of the pear tree. The fruit is of the size of a common grape, in which are similar small seeds. It ripens about the middle of autumn. The fruit is of a yellowish purple color, and it is too sweet to be agreeable to many people.

In the middle regions, on some of the prairies, large tracts are covered with the crab-apple tree.— Their appearance is like the cultivated apple tree, although the fruit and the tree are much smaller. It makes good cider and preserves, but is too tart to be eaten in its natural state.

The white and black mulberry are both found in the Mississippi valley, but the black is by far the most common. It has been satisfactorily proved, however, that the silk worm will thrive and produce well, upon the black mulberry.

Cane brake is seen on the banks of the Mississippi soon after you leave the mouth of the Ohio. It generally grows from fifteen to twenty feet in height; but in the rich bottoms near Natchez it sometimes attains the height of thirty feet. It is five years coming to maturity, and then produces an abundant crop of seed, on heads much resembling broom corn. It is an evergreen. The leaves are three or four inches long, but narrow and sharp pointed. It is much used for reeds and fishing rods. They grow so very thick that it is difficult for a man to make head way among them. When they are cut down and become dry, they burn freely.— The negroes have fine sport in burning them. The heat rarifies the air in the hollow between the joints and causes them to burst with a noise like a gun; so that when a large quantity of them are set on fire, the noise is like a continued discharge of musketry.

EXPENSES OF TRAVELLING.

BY WATER.

Cabin passage from Portsmouth to New Orleans	$25,00
From New Orleans to Texas	20,00
Total,	45,00

BY LAND.

Stage fare from Portsmouth to Brattleborough, Vt.	7,75
Albany	3,00
Railroad to Schenectady	,75
Line boat on the Canal to Buffalo and found	8,33
Cabin passage in a steamboat to Detroit	8,00
Stage fare to St. Joseph	9,50
Across the lake Michigan in a schooner to Chicago, Ill.	3,00
Stage fare to Peoria	9,50
Cabin passage in a steamboat to St. Louis, Mo.	7,00
Deck passage in steamboat to Natchez	7,00
From Natchez to the Colorado river—distance 521 miles— 20 days' travel on horseback at $1,25 per day	25,00
	88,83
Incidental expenses, probably	11,17
Total,	$100,00

I was about five months on my journey, and the whole expense was two hundred dollars. A single meal in the western and southern country is generally twenty-five cents; and the charge for supper, lodging, breakfast and horsekeeping was usually one dollar, where the new settlers pretended to keep a public house; but some of them would take nothing for what they furnished. Eastern bank bills are generally current in all the western country. In Texas, United States bank bills, bills of the New Orleans banks, and hard money are the only currency.

Distances from Portsmouth, N. H. to the Colorado river in Texas, by the way of Buffalo, St. Louis and Natchez.

From Portsmouth to Brattleborough	100	Roberts	20
Bennington	40	St. Augustine	5
Albany	40	Attoyac river	17
Schenectady	16	Morse's	12
Utica	80	Nacogdoches	13
Rochester	160	Total from Alexandria	
Lockport	63	to Nacogdoches	187
Buffalo	30		
Total from Portsmouth		Durst's	20
to Buffalo	529	Natches river	20
		Masters'	27
Detroit	305	Aldrich's	12
St. Joseph	200	Trinity river	15
Chicago, Ill.	60	Total from Nacogdoches	
Ottawa	80	to Trinity river	94
Peoria	80		
St. Louis	200	Anderson's	40
Total from Buffalo to		Hall's Ferry, Brazos,	30
St. Louis	925	Cole's Settlement	15
		Mitchel's	20
Mouth of the Ohio	180	Colorado river	35
Natchez	710	Total from the Trinity to	
Total from St. Louis		Colorado river	140
to Natchez	890		
		GRAND TOTAL,	2865
Tensaw	18		
Mathews	12		
Harrisonburg	12	From Portsmouth, N. H. to	
Alexandria	58	Texas by water.	
Total from Natchez			
to Alexandria	100	To New Orleans	2500
		Brazos river	500
Hendersons	25		
Fort Jessup	70	TOTAL,	3000
Sabine river	25		

The Far Western Frontier

An Arno Press Collection

[Angel, Myron, editor]. **History of Nevada.** 1881.

Barnes, Demas. **From the Atlantic to the Pacific, Overland.** 1866.

Beadle, J[ohn] H[anson]. **The Undeveloped West; Or, Five Years in the Territories.** [1873].

Bidwell, John. **Echoes of the Past:** An Account of the First Emigrant Train to California. [1914].

Bowles, Samuel. **Our New West.** 1869.

Browne, J[ohn] Ross. **Adventures in the Apache Country.** 1871.

Browne, J[ohn] Ross. **Report of the Debates in the Convention of California, on the Formation of the State Constitution.** 1850.

Byers, W[illiam] N. and J[ohn] H. Kellom. **Hand Book to the Gold Fields of Nebraska and Kansas.** 1859.

Carvalho, S[olomon] N. **Incidents of Travel and Adventure in the Far West; with Col. Fremont's Last Expedition Across the Rocky Mountains.** 1857.

Clayton, William. **William Clayton's Journal.** 1921.

Cooke, P[hilip] St. G[eorge]. **Scenes and Adventures in the Army.** 1857.

Cornwallis, Kinahan. **The New El Dorado; Or, British Columbia.** 1858.

Davis, W[illiam] W. H. **El Gringo; Or, New Mexico and Her People.** 1857.

De Quille, Dan. (William Wright). **A History of the Comstock Silver Lode & Mines.** 1889.

Delano, A[lonzo]. **Life on the Plains and Among the Diggings;** Being Scenes and Adventures of an Overland Journey to California. 1854.

Ferguson, Charles D. **The Experiences of a Forty-niner in California.** (Originally published as *The Experiences of a Forty-niner During Thirty-four Years' Residence in California and Australia*). 1888.

Forbes, Alexander. **California:** A History of Upper and Lower California. 1839.

Fossett, Frank. **Colorado:** Its Gold and Silver Mines, Farms and Stock Ranges, and Health and Pleasure Resorts. 1879.

The Gold Mines of California: Two Guidebooks. 1973.

Gray, W[illiam] H[enry]. **A History of Oregon, 1792–1849.** 1870.

Green, Thomas J. **Journal of the Texian Expedition Against Mier.** 1845.

Henry, W[illiam] S[eaton]. **Campaign Sketches of the War with Mexico.** 1847.

[Hildreth, James]. **Dragoon Campaigns to the Rocky Mountains.** 1836.

Hines, Gustavus. **Oregon:** Its History, Condition and Prospects. 1851.

Holley, Mary Austin. **Texas:** Observations, Historical, Geographical and Descriptive. 1833.

Hollister, Ovando J[ames]. **The Mines of Colorado.** 1867.

Hughes, John T. **Doniphan's Expedition.** 1847.

Johnston, W[illiam] G. **Experiences of a Forty-niner.** 1892.

Jones, Anson. **Memoranda and Official Correspondence Relating to the Republic of Texas, Its History and Annexation.** 1859.

Kelly, William. **An Excursion to California Over the Prairie, Rocky Mountains, and Great Sierra Nevada.** 1851. 2 Volumes in 1.

Lee, D[aniel] and J[oseph] H. Frost. **Ten Years in Oregon.** 1844.

Macfie, Matthew. **Vancouver Island and British Columbia.** 1865.

Marsh, James B. **Four Years in the Rockies; Or, the Adventures of Isaac P. Rose.** 1884.

Mowry, Sylvester. **Arizona and Sonora:** The Geography, History, and Resources of the Silver Region of North America. 1864.

Mullan, John. **Miners and Travelers' Guide to Oregon, Washington, Idaho, Montana, Wyoming, and Colorado.** 1865.

Newell, C[hester]. **History of the Revolution in Texas.** 1838.

Parker, A[mos] A[ndrew]. **Trip to the West and Texas.** 1835.

Pattie, James O[hio]. **The Personal Narrative of James O. Pattie, of Kentucky.** 1831.

Rae, W[illiam] F[raser]. **Westward by Rail:** The New Route to the East. 1871.

Ryan, William Redmond. **Personal Adventures in Upper and Lower California, in 1848–9.** 1850/1851. 2 Volumes in 1.

Shaw, William. **Golden Dreams and Waking Realities:** Being the Adventures of a Gold-Seeker in California and the Pacific Islands. 1851.

Stuart, Granville. **Montana As It Is:** Being a General Description of its Resources. 1865.

Texas in 1840, Or the Emigrant's Guide to the New Republic. 1840.

Thornton, J. Quinn. **Oregon and California in 1848.** 1849. 2 Volumes in 1.

Upham, Samuel C. **Notes of a Voyage to California via Cape Horn, Together with Scenes in El Dorado, in the Years 1849–'50.** 1878.

Woods, Daniel B. **Sixteen Months at the Gold Diggings.** 1851.

Young, F[rank] G., editor. **The Correspondence and Journals of Captain Nathaniel J. Wyeth, 1831–6.** 1899.